FAIRIES

·THE·FLOWER·FAIRY·IN·THE·MAGIC·GARRET·

FAIRIES

in legend & the arts

Alison Packer
Stella Beddoe
Lianne Jarrett

CAMERON & TAYLEUR
in association with
DAVID & CHARLES

Published by Cameron & Tayleur (Books) Limited, 25 Lloyd
Baker Street, London WC1X 9AT.
in association with David & Charles (Publishers) Limited, Brunel
House, Newton Abbot, Devon.
Distributed by David & Charles.

Text set by Input Typesetting, London, and Modern Text
Typesetting, Southend.
Colour reproduced by Gateway Platemakers, London, and printed
by Alan Moor, London.
Monochrome reproduced by Tenreck, London.
Monochrome printing and binding by R.J. Acford, Chichester.

Designed by Ian Cameron and Mrinalini Srivastava.
House editor: Norman Kolpas.

First published 1980.
Printed and bound in Great Britain.
ISBN 0 7153 8043 5

The authorship of the chapters is as follows: Introduction and Real
Fairies by Alison Packer; Fairies of Fiction and Fairy Painting and
Illustration by Stella Beddoe; Theatre by Lianne Jarrett.

ACKNOWLEDGEMENTS
This book represents the culmination of the research undertaken
for *Fairies*, The Brighton Festival Exhibition of 1980, which was
financed jointly by the Brighton Borough Council and the
Brighton Festival Society. A grant from South East Arts made it
possible to commission Fay Godwin to photograph the fairy sites
of Sussex. The authors would like to extend their thanks to all
those who gave their assistance: in particular, Dr Katharine
Briggs, Mr Jeremy Maas, Mr Henry Ford, Mr J.C. Trewin and Mr
John Gill. Without the cooperation of these authorities on
folklore, fairy paintings and the stage, this venture would have
been impossible.
    The publishers wish to thank the owners named in the captions
for permission to reproduce their pictures.

Frontispiece
Jessie M. King: *The Flower Fairy
in the Magic Garret*, 1903.
(Sunderland Museum and Art
Gallery)

Contents

List of Illustrations   6

Introduction   13

Real Fairies   21

Fairies of Fiction   44

Theatre   72

Fairy Painting and Illustration   110

Index   142

Bibliography   144

Illustrations

W. Heath Robinson: illustration to *Midsummer Night's Dream*, 1914. 8

Edmund Dulac: *Assemblage of Fairytale and Nursery Rhyme Characters.* 9

Sir Joseph Noel Paton: *The Fairy Raid*, 1867. 10

Walter Crane: Two pages from *A Floral Fantasy in an Old English Garden*, 1899. 12

John Atkinson Grimshaw: *Iris*, 1886. 13

Edith Graham; *Moonlit Scene with Fairies*, 1882. 14

Henry Thomas Ryall (after Sir Joseph Noel Paton): *The Pursuit of Pleasure* (detail). 15

The Luck of Eden Hall. 16

Wax Christmas tree fairy, c1900. 17

Costume made by Mrs Emily Meades for her daughter Eileen. 17

Richard Dadd: *Fairy's Rendezvous*, c1841. 18

Garden ornament — cross-legged pixie, designed by Harry Simeon and made by Royal Doulton, c1920. 18

H.R. Millar: *Puck of Pook's Hill*, illustration to Rudyard Kipling's book, 1906. 18

Anon: *Jack Courting the Fairy*, c1880. 19

Porcelain plate, enamel painted and gilded, after a design by Walter Crane used to illustrate *Flora's Feast*. 20

Richard Doyle: *The Fairy Minuet*, 1871. 21

Fay Godwin: Park Mound, Pulborough, Sussex. A Fairy funeral was once seen here. 22

Fay Godwin: Harrow Hill, Patching, Sussex — the fairies' last home in England was said to have been in the flint mines here. 23

Fay Godwin: a fairy site in Sussex — Tarberry Hill. 24

Fay Godwin: another fairy site in Sussex — Cissbury Ring. 25

Mary Corbett: illustration to James Hogg's *Kilmeny*, published 1845. 26

F.J. Wilcoxson: *Dryad*, 1925. 27

John Anster Fitzgerald: *Fairies' Banquet*, 1859. 28

Agostino Aglio: *Evening.* 30

David Scott: *The Belated Peasant.* 31

Two holed stone amulets. 32

Fairy Mirror, brass plate on a moulded handle. 32

Bronze age flint arrow heads, known as elf shot. 32

Robert Anning Bell: frontispiece for *A Midsummer Night's Dream*, 1895. 33

Robert Anning Bell: illustration to *A Midsummer Night's Dream*, 1895. 33

The Cottingley Fairies — photographs taken by Elsie Wright and Frances Griffiths in Cottingley, Yorkshire, between 1917 and 1920. Fairy offering flowers to Elsie, 1920. 34

Elsie and the gnome, 1917. 35

Frances and the fairies, 1917. 36

Watercolour by Elsie Wright: *Fairies beside a Stream.* 36

Miss Dorothy Inman: Fake fairy photograph. 37

William Marriot: photograph taken in 1921 in which he combined the fairies shown in the Price's advertisement with a photograph of Conan Doyle to demonstrate the possibility of producing a fake. 38

Watercolour by Elsie Wright: *Fairies flying over a cottage.* 39

Henry Hetherington Emmerson: illustration to Marion M. Wingrave's *The May Blossom or the Princess and Her People*, 1881. 40

Willy Pogány: *Peter Pan*, book illustration. 42

Richard Doyle: illustration to John Ruskin's *The King of the Golden River*, 1904. 43

Arthur Rackham: *The Widow Whitgift and her Sons.* Original illustration to *The Dymchurch Flit* from *Puck of Pook's Hill* by Rudyard Kipling, 1906. 45

John Anster Fitzgerald: *Ariel*, c1858-1868. 46

Arthur Rackham: *Elf Attendant on Bottom.* Original illustration to *A Midsummer Night's Dream*, 1908. 48

David Scott: *Puck Fleeing before the Dawn*, 1837. 49

Frontispiece to *Tom Pouce ou Le Petit Garçon*, translated from the English into French by Théodore-Pierre Bertin. 50

John Absalon: illustration to *Popular Nursery Tales including Tom Thumb*, c1860. 51

Kenny Meadows: illustration to *A Midsummer Night's Dream*, 1852. 52

John Simmons: *Titania.* 53

Richard Doyle: illustration to John Ruskin's *The King of the Golden River*, 1904. 53

Kenny Meadows: illustration to *A Midsummer Night's Dream*, 1852. 54

Kenny Meadows: illustration to *A Midsummer Night's Dream*, 1852. 55

Anon: illustration to *Sketches to Irish Characters*, 1855. 55

Illustration to Ludwig Bechstein's *Neues Deutsches Märchenbuch*, c1880. 56

Robert Huskisson: *There Sleeps Titania*, 1847. 58

Frederick Goodall: *Fairy Scene*, c1846. 59

Richard Doyle: *The Dance of the Pixies.* 61

Anon: illustration to *Beauty and the Beast* (attributed to Charles and Mary Lamb). 62

George Cruikshank: *Cinderella*, an etching from *Cruikshank's Fairy Library.* 63

General William John Chamberlayne: *Watersprites in a Stream*, c1865. 65

Willy Pogány: *Four Fairies Riding on Insects.* 65

William Thackeray: *The Fairy Blackstick*, illustration to the author's *The Rose and the Ring*, 1855. 68

Anon: Frontispiece to *Chat in the Playroom and Life at a Farmhouse*, c1870.   69

W.R. Ingram: *Ariel on the Bat's Back*.   71

Inigo Jones: *Oberon, The Fairy Prince*, costume design, 1611.   73

Miss Priscilla Horton as Ariel, *The Tempest*, The Theatre Royal Covent Garden, 1838.   75

Madame Vestris as Oberon, *A Midsummer Night's Dream*, The Theatre Royal Covent Garden, 1840.   76

Fairies dancing in the Palace of Theseus (Act V), *A Midsummer Night's Dream*. The Princess's Theatre, 1856.   77

The eight-year-old Ellen Terry seated on a mechanical mushroom, *A Midsummer Night's Dream*, 1856.   78

The Tempest, Last Scene, The Princess's Theatre, 1857. Engraving from the *Illustrated London Evening News*, 18th July 1857.   78

Miss Julia Neilson as Oberon, *A Midsummer Night's Dream*, Her Majesty's Theatre, 1900.   79

Loudon Sainthill: *A Sea Creature*, costume design for *The Tempest*, Shakespeare Memorial Theatre, Stratford upon Avon, 1952.   81

Francis Danby: *Scene from A Midsummer Night's Dream*, 1832.   82

Edmund Dulac: She found herself face to face with a stately and beautiful lady, original drawing for *Beauty and the Beast*, 1910.   84

Puck and a Fairy, *A Midsummer Night's Dream*, The Savoy Theatre, 1914.   85

Michael Fokine rehearsing the fairy ballets for *A Midsummer Night's Dream*, The Theatre Royal, Drury Lane, 1924. Double page spread from the *Illustrated London News*, 27th December 1924.   86

Vivien Leigh as Titania, Ralph Richardson as Bottom, and Robert Helpmann as Oberon in *A Midsummer Night's Dream*, The Old Vic Theatre, 1937.   87

Marius Goring as Ariel, *The Tempest*, The Old Vic Theatre, 1940.   88

Margaret Leighton as Ariel, *The Tempest*, Stratford upon Avon, 1952.   89

A scene from Peter Brook's production of *A Midsummer Night's Dream*, 1970.   90

John Gielgud as Prospero, Michael Feast as Ariel in Peter Hall's production of *The Tempest*, The Old Vic Theatre, 1974.   91

Robert Helpmann as Oberon, costume design by Michael Ayrton, *The Fairy Queen*, The Royal Opera House, Covent Garden, 1946.   92

A scene from Benjamin Britten's *A Midsummer Night's Dream*, designed by John Piper, The Royal Opera House, Covent Garden, 1961.   94

Anthony Dowell as Oberon in Sir Frederick Ashton's *The Dream*, The Royal Opera House, Covent Garden, 1979.   95

Playbill for the first production of *Oberon: or the Elf King's Oath*, at Covent Garden, music by Carl Maria von Weber, 12th April 1826.   97

Scenes from the first production of Gilbert and Sullivan's *Iolanthe*, the Savoy Theatre, 1882. Picture from *The Graphic*.   98

Charles Wilhelm: costume design for one of the twelve Fairy Godmothers in *Sleeping Beauty*, 1886.   100

Grand Transformation Scene from *The Island of Jewels*, 1849.   101

Marie Taglioni as La Sylphide, lithograph by J.H. Lynch from a drawing by A.E. Chalon, 1845.   102

Lucile Grahn in *Eoline ou la Dryade*, lithography by Edward Morton after S.M. Joy, 1845.   103

Margot Fonteyn as Cinderella, Annette Page as the Fairy Godmother, David Blair as the Prince in *Cinderella*, Covent Garden, 1965.   104

Carlotta Brianza as Carabosse in *The Sleeping Princess*, The Alhambra, 1921.   105

Margot Fonteyn and Robert Helpmann in *Sleeping Beauty*, Act II, Covent Garden, 1946.   106

Peter Schaufuss, Vivien Loeber and Eva Evdokimova in *Les Sylphides*, London Festival Ballet, 1976.   107

Eleanor Fortescue Brickdale: *The Lovers' World*, 1905. 108

Villanis: *Farfalla*, The title derives from a corruption of 'firefly'.   109

Fairies Dancing, an illustration from an old English chapbook.   110

Henry Fuseli: *Titania and Bottom*, 1875.   112

Daniel Maclise: *The Faun and the Fairies*, c1834.   113

W. Blake: *Oberon, Titania and Puck with Fairies dancing*. 114

G. Cruikshank: *The Elves and the Shoemaker*, illustration to *German Popular Stories*, 1823.   114

Daniel Maclise: illustration to Dickens's *The Chimes*, c1845.   116

Sir Joseph Noel Paton: *The Reconciliation of Oberon and Titania*, 1847.   116

George Cruikshank: etching from Thomas Keightley's *Fairy Mythology*, 1828.   118

Richard Doyle: illustration to Mark Lemon's *The Enchanted Doll*, 1849.   119

E. Griset: illustration to Lord Brabourne's *The Little Gentleman*.   120

Richard Doyle: *A Fairy Ring*.   121

Robert Huskisson: *The Mother's Blessing*.   122

John Simmons: *Scene from A Midsummer Night's Dream*, Act III scene 1, 'The honey-bags steal from the humble bees'.   123

Thomas Heatherley: *Fairy seated on a Mushroom*.   124

William Shackleton: *The Nymph of Malham Cove*, 'Moonlight Idyll'.   125

Richard Dadd: *Songe de la Fantasie*, 1864.   126

Richard Doyle: *Sprites on a Cliff*.   127

John Anster Fitzgerald: *Fairies in a Bird's Nest*.   128

Richard Doyle: illustration to *Dick Doyle's Journal*, 1885.   128

Arthur Hughes: illustration to Christina Rossetti's *Sing Song, A Nursery Rhyme Book*, 1872.   129

Arthur Hughes: illustration to Christina Rossetti's *Sing Song, A Nursery Rhyme Book*.   129

Arthur Hughes: illustration to Christina Rossetti's *Sing Song, A Nursery Rhyme Book*.   130

Dante Gabriel Rossetti: detail from title page to Christina Rossetti's *Goblin Market and Other Poems*, 1865.   130

Dante Gabriel Rossetti: 'The Maids of Elfen Mere', illustration to William Allingham's *The Music Masters, a love story and two series of Day and Night Songs*, 1855.   131

H.J. Ford: 'The Hobgoblin laughed till his sides ached', illustration to *The Snow-Queen*, from *The Pink Fairy Book* edited by Andrew Lang, 1901.   132

Eleanor Vere Boyle: *When the Spring Begins* from Carové's *The Story without an End*, 1868.   133

Richard Doyle: *Triumphal march of the Elf-King* from *In Fairyland* by William Allingham, 1870.   134

Daisy Makeig Jones: bone chine plaque, c1917, Wedgwood Fairyland Lustre.   136

Charles Robinson: *Fairy in an Autumn Glade*.   137

Frederick Cayley Robinson: 'The Dance of the Hours', illustration to the Methuen Edition of Maeterlinck's *The Bluebird*, 1911.   138

Arthur Rackham: 'Midsummer Fairies', illustration to *Lamb's Tales from Shakespeare*, 1899.   138

W. Heath Robinson: illustrations to Act V (*above*) and Act III, scene ii (*right*) from *A Midsummer Night's Dream*, 1914.   139

John Dicksen Batten: 'Connia and the Fairy Maid', illustration for Jacob's *Celtic Fairy Tales*, 1892.   140

Mabel Lucie Attwell: illustration from *The Boo Boos at the Seaside*, c1920.   140

Charles Rennie Mackintosh: *Fairies*, 1898.   141

W. Heath Robinson: illustration to *Midsummer Night's Dream*, 1914.

Edmund Dulac: *Assemblage of Fairytale and Nursery Rhyme Characters*. (British Museum)

Overleaf
Sir Joseph Noel Paton: *The Fairy Raid*, 1867. (Glasgow Museum and Art Gallery)

There's
TRAVELLER'S
JOY
To entwine,
At our
journeys end
for greeting,

Single Daisies
were not
in her eye,

For
the grass
was just
newly mown.

Introduction

Walter Crane: Two pages from
*A Floral Fantasy in an Old English
Garden*, 1899

How did the lordly Oberon of Shakespeare's *A Midsummer
Night's Dream*, dwindle into J. M. Barrie's Tinkerbell, who
can be extinguished by mere lack of belief? Our aim here
is to trace and explain the changing character and appearance of fairies in the British Isles, in folklore and legend,
literature and art, from their earliest recorded mention in
the 12th century up to the present day. We also include a
survey of fairy representations on the British stage, in plays,
operas, ballets and pantomimes.

Not wishing to trespass on the traditions of other coun-
tries, we have limited ourselves to indigenous fairies, while
admitting that some British fairy legends or tales may have
origins in other lands. Gnomes, which are so often wrongly
grouped together with fairies, will not concern us here.
They are, in fact, another species altogether, first described

John Atkinson Grimshaw: *Iris*,
1886. (Leeds City Art Gallery)

13

by the physician and alchemist Paracelsus (1493–1531) in *De Nymphis*: creatures of scientific theory, elementals which are the embodiment of earth and supposedly able to move through it as easily as mortals through air.

Edith Graham: *Moonlit Scene with Fairies,* 1882. (Alister Mathew, Bournemouth)

The word fairy itself most probably derives from the Latin *fatae*—the Fates. Fay-erie meant at first a state of enchantment, but then shifted in meaning to signify the creatures responsible for that enchantment. In early writings the word 'elf' is found more often; Chaucer, for example, uses it in *The Wife of Bath's Tale*. Fairy is used here in its broadest possible sense to embrace all supernatural creatures, such as goblins, hobgoblins, brownies, boggarts, bogles, sprites and even mer-people. Similar creatures occur in tales and descriptions from all over the British Isles, under different names according to the area, but generally with many characteristics in common.

In the accounts of actual sightings that have come down to us, the word fairy is seldom used. Fairies were and are more often spoken of placatingly as the Good People, the Gentry or the People of Peace. Their love of secrecy and privacy is usually respected by those anxious not to offend them; they can avenge themselves viciously on those who trespass on their kindness, or who betray a trust. One example of folk legend will suffice to illustrate this point.

The story of a midwife to the fairies is very common throughout the country, and its elements are always the same. A human midwife is summoned in the middle of the night to deliver a baby in a house nearby. Before she enters the house, she is told to smear an ointment on her eyes. When she crosses the threshold, she finds herself in a beautiful mansion with marvellous decorations and sumptuous hangings. Having safely delivered the child, she accidentally rubs one eye with her sleeve, thus removing the ointment. With that eye she then sees the house as it really is, a squalid hovel, and the people she has been attending as small, oddly shaped fairies. She says nothing and makes her way home. Shortly afterwards, she meets the fairy husband and asks after his new child. 'With which eye do you see me?' he enquires. She tells him. Straightaway he blinds her in that eye, and disappears. The ointment was fairy 'glamour', a charm to disguise reality

Henry Thomas Ryall (after Sir Joseph Noel Paton): *The Pursuit of Pleasure* (detail). (A.R.E. North)

There are many more tales of traffic with the fairies, both here on earth and in Fairyland. In some tales, men and women receive gifts from the fairies; but more often, to the discredit of the human race, there are thefts from Fairyland. The most famous reputed example of such booty is the Luck of Edenhall, an exotic glass cup decorated with enamel. The butler of the Musgrave family of Edenhall, in Cumberland, was said to have stolen the cup from a fairy picnic he encountered, and rode away with it back to the Hall. Unable to regain it, the fairies shouted after him,

> If this cup should break or fall,
> Farewell the Luck of Edenhall.

The Luck of Eden Hall
(Victoria and Albert Museum)

Fortunately, the glass remains intact to this day. It was in the possession of the Musgrave family until 1926, when it was offered on loan to the Victoria & Albert Museum, which formally acquired it in 1958. It seems that the glass is actually of Syrian origin, made in the mid-13th century, and was possibly brought home by a crusader.

It is obvious from such stories that fairies have not always been the tiny, sparkling but impotent creatures of the sort represented at the top of present-day Christmas trees. This recent embodiment is only one strand in the complex skein of legend, folklore and literature which makes up the fairy tradition. It is sometimes difficult to separate the genuine folk tradition from the results of centuries of literary invention and conceit. Through literature, the vigorous country elves and fairies of folk tradition were gradually transformed into the charming but powerless fairies most familiar to modern children. The process began in the 16th century. From the wealth of fairy tradition available as a source of inspiration to the poets and dramatists of that time, it was the mischievous and the miniature qualities of these creatures that were singled out for the most attention. The mischievous aspect was embodied by the character of Robin Goodfellow (Puck, as he appears in Shakespeare) who was, it will be remembered, given to changing shape, taunting old farmers' wives, tripping up night wanderers and generally misbehaving to the huge amusement of the rest of the fairy kingdom. The other, more delicate, aspect was represented by the Fairy King and Queen, who had many of the qualities of mortal monarchs. In the 17th century, the miniaturist poets occupied the centre of the stage. They vied with one another to produce lists of yet more microscopic items to furnish their impossible Fairylands. The miniaturisation process frequently diminished the power of fairies who once wielded great influence over man and nature—who could, like the ancient gods, change the seasons, and put the country

Wax Christmas tree fairy, c1900. (Miss Yootha Rose)

Costume made by Mrs Emily Meades for her daughter Eileen. (Oxfordshire County Museum)

calendar out of joint, as Titania proclaims to Oberon in *A Midsummer Night's Dream*:

... the spring, the summer,
The chiding autumn, angry winter change
Their wonted liveries; and the maz'd world,
By their increase, now knows not which is which:
And this same progeny of evils come
From our debate, from our dissension:
We are their parents and original.

The external appearance of fairies has altered a great deal over the eight centuries since the first written descriptions of them appeared. Nowadays, most people asked to describe a fairy would begin with the wings. Curiously enough, however, wings are a comparatively recent development. In the early chronicles, or in early literature, there are hardly any fairies with wings. Fairies have certainly always flown, although generally without the use of wings. If the fairies were small, they could ride on a bird, or on a bat's back like Ariel. Alternatively, they could call out a magic password. 'Horse and Hattock' was a favourite, reported by John Aubrey among others, and was known to work sometimes for humans as well.

Wings were most probably introduced as a result of reverse logic: fairies are known to have flown, and therefore must have had wings. The appearance of these wings, and often of the fairies themselves, owes much to other visual traditions. There are, first of all, the butterfly-type wings. This form comes ultimately from Greek art, in which the soul, or Psyche, was often shown as a miniature human with butterfly wings. This image turns up frequently on Greek pots, in particular on white-ground *lekythoi*, which were frequently made to be put into tombs and were illustrated, therefore, with symbols of death and the passage of the soul into the after-life.

This image was taken up again in the Renaissance, which saw a revival of classical forms and the retelling of classical legends. The story of Cupid and Psyche was especially popular. It appears in the loggia of the Villa Farnesina in Rome, which Raphael decorated for a wealthy banker in the early 16th century. On the ceiling is shown the wedding feast of Cupid and Psyche, who are attended by three naked women with butterfly wings. They are the precursors of the well-endowed, naked female fairies of Victorian painting. Another source is the small cupids of Greek and Roman sculpture. These were adapted to a Christian context as *putti* (cherubs) in the Renaissance, and then put back into the pagan world by later fairy illustrators. The *putti* of 15th century painting and sculpture are the distant cousins of the infant fairies of the early

17

Richard Dadd: *Fairy's Rendezvous, c*1841. (Walker Art Gallery, Liverpool)

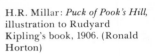

H.R. Millar: *Puck of Pook's Hill,* illustration to Rudyard Kipling's book, 1906. (Ronald Horton)

Garden ornament—cross-legged pixie, designed by Harry Simeon and made by Royal Doulton, *c*1920. (Barbara Morris)

Anon: *Jack Courting the Fairy,*
*c*1880. (Michael Heseltine)

20th century.

The other major source for the appearance of fairy wings is the Bible. Fairies do, from time to time, appear with feathered wings such as angels have. The famous Christmas tree fairy, of German origin, surely derives from an angel. Fairies themselves were often thought to be fallen angels, so the iconography is in this case particularly appropriate.

Fairy painting borrows from these other visual traditions and is more closely allied to literary creations than to folklore. Shakespeare is of enormous importance. Many, many paintings were inspired by *A Midsummer Night's Dream*, but with elements added from other sources and from the artists' imagination. Such heroic examples of fairies in art, however, could not continue; as in literature, so in painting the fairies were diminished under the miniaturist influence. The Tinkerbells and flower fairies of the early 20th century are direct descendents of the fantasies of Herrick and the Duchess of Newcastle. Rudyard Kipling, in *Puck of Pook's Hill*, tried valiantly to restore to some extent the vigour of the old tradition, but without too much success. The delicate fairies portrayed by such artists as Mabel Lucie Attwell, Margaret Tarrant and Cecily Mary Barker had taken hold of the popular imagination.

Nevertheless, some artists did manage to create genuine fairy worlds of their own, separate from almost all traditions. Richard Dadd and John Anster Fitzgerald are the best examples. The huge output of fairy painting and illustration, whether heroic or delicate, produced in the 19th

century in its turn provided a rich source of inspiration for the decorative arts, especially for ceramics. Fairies appeared on all manner of things, from tiles to complete tea services, and the pieces continue to be extremely popular and greatly sought after by collectors. The current wave of reprintings of fairy books and illustrations demonstrates the continuing fascination which the subject exercises, even in the late 20th century. Mankind's conception of fairies may have changed, but his delight, and sometimes belief, in them persists.

Porcelain plate, enamel painted and gilded, after a design by Walter Crane used to illustrate *Flora's Feast*

Real Fairies

A belief in other worlds, inhabited by spiritual beings, which sometimes come into contact with our own, has always existed. The earliest surviving written accounts of fairy encounters date from the 12th century, but, of course, the tradition is very much older. Many of the fairies encountered in chronicles and traditional tales have qualities in common. They can be roughly divided into three major types. First are the grand, or 'heroic', fairies. They are of about human size and inhabit Fairyland, a sort of parallel country where time passes at a different rate from this world and where occasionally humans visit, or are imprisoned. Sometimes they live in fairy knolls, or ancient barrows and other archaeological sites. They dance, feast,

Richard Doyle: *The Fairy Minuet,* 1871. (Private collection, Maas Gallery photograph)

21

Fay Godwin: Park Mound, Pulborough, Sussex. A fairy funeral was once seen here.

and live in many ways as we do, only on a grander scale.

Next, there are the so-called 'Trooping Fairies', of whom Oberon and Titania are the most famous literary examples. They rule their fairy kingdom in much the same way as human kings and queens, and are generally helpful to humans. Sometimes, however, they can be mischievous, and even on occasion steal from mortals. They use 'elf-shot' against cattle, and are able somehow to extract the goodness from milk or barley, leaving it apparently untouched but in reality worthless. They also steal human babies, substituting either a block of wood or a particularly ancient and unattractive fairy as a changeling. Trooping fairies can be kept at bay with various devices including fairy stones (stones with natural holes in them) and iron. They have markets, celebrations and, very occasionally, funerals. There is some dispute about whether such fairies are all immortal, but a fairy funeral was once seen on Pulborough Mount in Sussex.

Finally, there are the more humble fairies: brownies, hobgoblins and the like. They dress in ragged clothes, or occasionally in no clothes at all, and enjoy performing household tasks. They must be treated with great care and not offended, or they can turn into malevolent spirits.

In 1188, Giraldus Cambrensis made a journey through Wales in an attempt to drum up support for the Third Crusade. He described the journey in his chronicle *Itinerarium Cambriae* (translated in Penguin Classics). A learned man, he collected a wide variety of information and stories from the people he encountered, and it is in his writing that we find one of the earliest recorded tales connected

Fay Godwin: Harrow Hill, Patching, Sussex — the fairies' last home in England was said to have been in the flint mines here.

with fairies, 'Elidor and the Golden Ball', which describes a twelve-year-old boy's visit to Fairyland.

The story was told to Giraldus by a priest who insisted that the experience was his own. Giraldus himself was not entirely convinced of the truth of this tale, but he resolved to keep an open mind. He describes the events as happening 'a short time before our days', and the story is particularly valuable for the information it gives about the fairies themselves. They were small and fair-haired, and lived in a beautiful country reached by travelling underground. They were a vegetarian race, spoke a language similar to ancient Greek and were ruled by a King. There seemed to be no religion or moral code, except that the fairies valued the truth above all else. It is worth noting that, in common with other fairies of these early chronicles, those seen by

Fay Godwin: a fairy site in Sussex—Tarberry Hill.

Fay Godwin: another fairy site in Sussex — Cissbury Ring.

Elidor had no wings.

A contemporary of Giraldus, Gervase of Tilbury, also describes small fairies in his work *Otia Imperiali*, which was finished in 1211. These he called the 'Portunes', who were evidently different from the creatures encountered by Elidor. They looked like wrinkled old men, wore ragged garments, and were found in the country, helping in agricultural labours, rather than far away in Fairyland. Gervase records that the Portunes were only half an inch in height. It is possible, however, that through a copyist's error their size was reduced further than the author intended; Gervase also reports that they carried frogs about to roast on the embers of farmhouse fires, for which task they would have required considerably more height than half an inch.

Mary Corbett: illustration to
James Hogg's *Kilmeny*,
published 1845. (Raymond
Watkinson)

Not all early descriptions of fairies show them as tiny
creatures. Sometimes they are the same height, if not taller,
than humans. The story of Wild Edric, told by Walter
Map, another 12th century chronicler, in *De Nugis Curialium*, describes the fairies encountered by Edric. From
them he chooses his bride, a woman larger than human
women and of greater beauty.

The great beauty of fairy women is stressed again in the
story of True Thomas or Thomas the Rhymer. Thomas
Rymour of Erceldoune, who lived in the 13th century, met
one day a very beautiful woman whom he immediately
took to be the Virgin Mary. She was, in fact, the Queen of
Elfland. The story of Thomas's visit to Elfland with the
Queen, which lasted seven years, is told in several ballads,
which were not collected and published until much later.
When Thomas left Elfland, the Queen made him a present
of truthfulness, and ever afterwards he was known as True
Thomas.

Another early account in which the fairies are of human size is the strange story of the 'Green Children' recounted by both Ralph of Coggleshall and William of Newbridge, two monastic chroniclers. Two children, a boy and a girl, were discovered in a village in Suffolk. Although exactly like human children in all other respects, they had green skin. When first found, they would eat nothing but green beans, and were unable to say where they had come from. The boy soon died, but the girl lived, and grew up and gradually lost her green complexion. She later declared that everyone in the place she had come from was green in colour. (The colour green appears constantly in fairy stories, although generally the fairies have green clothes rather than green skin.)

F.J. Wilcoxson: *Dryad,* 1925.
(Williamson Art Gallery and
Museum, Wirral, Merseyside)

Occasionally, fairies are described as being of very much more than human size. At the beginning of this century, one Irishman described them as being about 14 feet tall and 'opalescent'. However, by far the most sightings have been of small creatures.

The 16th and 17th centuries saw the publication of an enormous amount of literature with a fairy theme. *A Midsummer Night's Dream* may have been the most important, but it was only one of the many poems, plays, masques and allegories inspired by the fairy tradition. Much of the literature is charming but fanciful, owing more to the poetic imagination than to folk lore. Shakespeare used some more traditional elements in *A Midsummer Night's Dream*, particularly Puck, or Robin Goodfellow, who has a very respectable country provenance. Herrick's courtly concoctions, however, leave real fairies far behind. Nevertheless, reports of sightings of, and encounters with, fairies continued throughout these centuries, and are more akin to the medieval chronicles than to the creations of contemporary poets and playwrights.

The 17th-century diarist, John Aubrey noted many fairy stories in his writings. He tells how, when he was a boy at school in Wiltshire, around 1633, the local curate was tormented by fairies when walking home late one night. The curate described them as 'pigmies, or very small people'. Once he had stumbled unawares into the fairy ring, he was pinched and pulled and unable to escape until the morning, when the creatures disappeared.

In 1645, a Cornishwoman, Anne Jeffries, declared that she had visited Fairyland itself. Furthermore, she manifested some powers of clairvoyance as proof of her visit. The fairies she encountered were very small—small enough to stand on the palm of her hand—and were dressed in green. As soon as she had entered Fairyland, though, they no longer seemed so tiny, and appeared to be of human size.

Many similar reports were collected in the 17th century but the 18th century was apparently less interested in common folklore. Writers, instead, made up Fairy Godmothers and similar characters in improving literature for children. The poet, William Blake, however, was an interesting exception to this rule. He believed he witnessed a fairy funeral in his back garden. The fairies he saw were the size of grasshoppers, and used a rose leaf as a bier. More corporeal creatures were to be found exhibited among the monsters and prodigies, the reports of which were collected by Henry Morley and published in his *Memoirs of Bartholomew Fair* in 1859. One could, for example, have seen, as a handbill announced, 'a living FAIRY, supposed to be a hundred and fifty years old, his face being no bigger than

John Anster Fitzgerald: *Fairies' Banquet*, 1859. (Private Collection, Maas Gallery photograph)

a child's of a month: was found sixty years ago; looked as old then as he does now. His head being a great piece of curiosity, having no skull, with several imperfections worthy of your observation.' The principal feature of these unfortunate creatures seems to have been their smallness. They certainly attracted great crowds, who were willing to pay as much as two shillings and sixpence to look at them. Another handbill described a changeling child which was to be seen at the time of the Fair at the Black Raven

Agostino Aglio: *Evening.*
(Private collection, Maas
Gallery photograph)

Tavern in West Smithfield. This fairy child was 'aged nine years and more, not exceeding a foot and a half high. The legs, thighs and arms so very small, that they scarce exceed the bigness of a man's thumb, and the face no bigger than the palm of one's hand; and seems so grave and solid as if it were threescore years old. It never speaks. It has no teeth, but it is the most voracious and hungry creature in the world, devouring more victuals than the stoutest man in England.' Fairy encounters obviously did not cease with the age of Reason, and entrepreneurs were only too ready to make money out of the credulity of the public.

The 19th century saw a revival of interest in the collection and publication of genuine, ancient folktales and traditions of the British Isles. With the revival came a new desire to explain and understand fairies or the belief in their existence. There is no single, satisfactory explanation for the growth and persistence of belief in fairies in Britain, or indeed in any other country. However, several theories do emerge regularly from the early descriptions and from the welter of research undertaken from the 19th century onwards by earnest folklorists and social scientists. The answer, if there is one, may well include elements from all the different theories.

The most common theory equates fairies with the souls of the dead (pre-Christian dead for the most part) and

Fairyland with the place where the souls wait, with varying degrees of patience, for the Last Judgment, at which time all souls will be reunited with their bodies. Widespread examples exist. In the Highlands of Scotland, the 'Sluagh', or 'Host', who ride through the sky at night, fighting vicious battles and staining the earth with their crimson blood, are the souls of the unforgiven dead; they cannot enter Heaven until atonement is made for the sins they have committed on earth. In Cornwall, the Small People are the souls of those who died before Christ, and are too good for Hell, but not good enough for Heaven. They are condemned to roam the earth, gradually diminishing in size, until in the end they disappear completely. The small size of these fairies is consistent with the traditional belief that the soul of a man was a tiny version of the man himself.

The theory of fairies as lost souls is linked to the idea of Fairyland as the equivalent of Hades, the mythical underworld ruled by Pluto and Persephone, where no food or drink may be consumed by the living visitor lest he be compelled to remain there forever. In the medieval romance *King Orfeo*, an adaptation of the Orpheus story, Pluto becomes the Fairy King, and it is to Fairyland that Orpheus must go to reclaim Eurydice (which, incidentally, he does without mishap). Slightly later, Chaucer, in *The Wife of Bath's Tale*, calls the Fairy Queen Persephone. There are countless fairy and folk tales dealing with visitors to, and captives in Fairyland, and the taboo against eating and drinking there. The theory seems to combine pre-Christian ideas of the underworld of the dead with Christian ones of the Last Judgment and Heaven.

David Scott: *The Belated Peasant.* (National Gallery of Scotland, Edinburgh)

Another popular theory for the belief in fairies is a more anthropological one. At the end of the 19th century, David MacRitchie, a member of the Folk-Lore Society, postulated a primitive, pigmy race of ancient Britons in his studies *The Testimony of Tradition* (1890) and *Fians, Fairies and Picts* (1893). These beings lived in the British Isles until they were driven into hiding by invaders from abroad; they skulked around at twilight and were frequently mistaken by country people for supernatural beings. They would have lived in caves or in dwellings disguised as mounds of earth, thus creating the idea of fairy knolls or howes so frequently mentioned in early reports of fairy sightings. In support of this theory, it is certainly true that neolithic arrow heads were frequently taken for fairy arrows, or 'elf-shot', which could apparently cause injury to cattle or men without piercing the skin. Some of the ancient race MacRitchie described perhaps became more domesticated, and furnished the prototype of the brownie or household fairy, rather ugly and dishevelled but nonetheless willing and mostly benevolent. There was hot debate when MacRitchie's theory was discussed by the Folk-Lore Society in 1891, but nothing was resolved. Again, it is very likely that there are elements of truth in what he said, but it is certainly not the whole story. It has been thought that fairies might also derive from folk memories of the Druids and their magical practices, but this seems less convincing.

Another suggestion is that fairies are fallen angels, wandering the earth because they have been denied access to both Heaven and Hell. The belief seems to have been most widespread in Ireland, where fairies have been viewed as gentle and beautiful creatures. Fairies were sometimes seen, however, as no better than devils, particularly by the Puritans. The connection between fairies and evil spirits was often made in 16th and 17th century witch trials, when

Fairy Mirror, brass plate on a moulded handle. (Highland Folk Museum, Kingussie)

Robert Anning Bell: illustrations to *A Midsummer Night's Dream*, 1895. (Victoria and Albert Museum)

Overleaf
The Cottingley Fairies — photographs taken by Elsie Wright and Frances Griffiths in Cottingley, Yorkshire, between 1917 and 1920. Fairy offering flowers to Elsie, 1920. (The Brotherton Collection, University of Leeds)

Elsie and the gnome, 1917. (The Brotherton Collection, University of Leeds)

Two holed stone amulets. (Towneley Hall Art Gallery and Museums, Burnley)

Bronze age flint arrow heads, known as elf shot. (Royal Pavilion, Art Gallery and Museums, Brighton)

young women practising white as well as black magic confessed to knowledge of Fairyland and the Fairy Queen, although they generally denied that there was any evil in it. Such denials were, however, of no avail, and many were executed.

It has also been suggested that fairies are purely creatures of the imagination, created by our credulous forefathers to explain seemingly inexplicable natural phenomena in the same way as the ancient gods and goddesses personified the earth or the sun, thunder or lightning. Alternatively, they are memories of those very pagan gods, diminished both in stature and powers but never quite vanishing.

Finally, it is possible that fairies are none of these, but a real race of invisible or spiritual beings unlike any other creature in all respects, but with similarities to several, such as ghosts, angels and devils. Robert Kirk, a minister of the Scottish church, described them in 1691 in *The Secret Commonwealth of Elves, Fauns and Fairies*, as '. . . of a middle nature betwixt Man and Angel . . . of intelligent, studious spirits, and light changeable bodies . . . somewhat of the nature of a condensed cloud, and best seen at twilight.'

In the early 20th century, the first attempts were made to record fairies (whatever their origin) in a new way, through photography. The first photographs ever to show fairies were taken in July 1917 by two young girls, Elsie Wright, then aged 15, and her cousin Frances Griffiths, aged 11, in Cottingley, Yorkshire. The first two pictures showed Frances with a dancing group of fairies, and Elsie in conversation with a goblin. Elsie's father remained sceptical about the photographs, but in May 1920, a friend of the family, who was a Theosophist, sent the two prints to E. L. Gardner, a Theosophist with a special interest in the subject. He in turn, contacted Sir Arthur Conan Doyle, who had similar interests. Thereafter, a great deal of correspondence passed between these two eminent men and the small Yorkshire town.

34

Frances and the fairies, 1917.
(The Brotherton Collection,
University of Leeds)

Watercolour by Elsie Wright:
Fairies beside a Stream. (The
Brotherton Collection,
University of Leeds)

Miss Dorothy Inman: Fake fairy photograph. (The Brotherton Collection, University of Leeds)

Conan Doyle was writing an article for the Strand Magazine at the time about evidence for the belief in fairies, and so was particularly fascinated when he saw the prints. He was convinced that they were genuine, and wrote about them in his book *The Coming of the Fairies*, published in 1922. Gardner arranged for a further three photographs to be taken by Elsie under controlled conditions, and more fairies duly appeared on the plates.

William Marriot: photograph taken in 1921 in which he combined the fairies shown in the Price's advertisement (see above) with a photograph of Conan Doyle to demonstrate the possibility of producing a fake. (Mary Evans Picture Library, Harry Price Collection, University of London)

Watercolour by Elsie Wright: *Fairies flying over a cottage.* (The Brotherton Collection, University of Leeds)

So far, there has been no convincing explanation of how the results were achieved. A professional photographer approached by Gardner was reasonably convinced by the photographs, but experts at Kodak, who were called upon to give a second opinion, expressed their doubts about the enterprise. Elsie was a competent watercolourist, and examples of her fairy paintings are very similar to the fairies that she photographed. Modern theories include the suggestion that the Cottingley fairies are projected thought forms, which would explain why Elsie's watercolour fairies should be so like those in the photographs. On the other hand, it is certainly possible to fake a photograph which looks very like the Cottingley pictures. Miss Dorothy

Henry Hetherington Emmerson: illustration to Marion M. Wingrave's *The May Blossom or the Princess and Her People,* 1881. (Ronald Horton)

Inman produced just such a photograph shortly after the Cottingley episode, but unfortunately died without revealing her secret. Sixty years after the event, the Cottingley mystery remains intact.

Well into this century, fairies have continued to make appearances, if one cares to look for them. The fairy tradition is still particularly strong in Scotland and Ireland. In his book *Ancestral Voices*, published in 1975, James Lees-Milne recorded a conversation he had with the Duke of Argyll in the early 1940s:

> At tea the Duke talked of fairies in whom he implicitly believes, as do all the people here. He described them as the spirits of a race of men who ages ago lived in earth mounds, which are what they frequent. They are usually little green things that peer at you from behind trees, as squirrels do, and disappear into the earth. The Duke has visited numerous fairy haunts in Argyll. So has his sister, Lady Elspeth, who at dinner one night announced with solemnity, 'The fairies are out in their sieves tonight.' 'Crossing over to Ireland no doubt,' her brother replied. 'We are not good enough for them in Scotland. Why! last year at Tipperary there were so many of them that they caused a traffic block.'

Very recently, a woman interviewed in The Guardian declared that she often saw and heard fairies. Their voices, she said, were like a speeded-up tape recording. She lives not in a remote Highland village, but in west London. Her matter-of-fact belief differs little from the attitude recounted a century ago by W. B. Yeats in his introduction to *Irish Fairy and Folk Tales*:

> 'Have you ever seen a fairy or such like?' I asked the old man in County Sligo. 'Amn't I annoyed with them' was the answer. 'Do the fishermen along here know anything of the mermaids?' I asked a woman of a village in County Dublin. 'Indeed they don't like to see them at all' she answered, 'for they always bring bad weather.'

Admittedly, in our modern world, experiences similar to those found in the early accounts of fairy sightings are more likely to be explained in a different way. What was once attributed to the fairies is now ascribed to UFOs or to aliens from other planets. It is interesting to note, however, that it seems that the experiences themselves have altered little; lights in the sky at night, the meeting with small 'opalescent' creatures, bodily transportation and the like, continue to be described by people all over the world. The only difference is that 20th century man thinks in terms of science fiction rather than folk tradition.

Willy Pogány: *Peter Pan,* book   Gallery and Museums, Burnley)
illustration. (Towneley Hall Art

Richard Doyle: illustration to   *Golden River*, 1904. (Ronald
John Ruskin's *The King of the*   Horton)

Fairies of Fiction

From earliest times, people have told one another stories of magic and enchantment. At first, the supernatural seemed to offer the only solutions to the mysterious and perplexing problems that man encountered in his dealings with others and with the universe. But even after the arrival of Christianity in the British Isles, the idea of an older race, endowed with magical powers, not answerable to human laws but nonetheless able to influence the course of mortal lives, continued to exercise its fascination. As belief diminished in the actual powers wielded by the fairies, so the fanciful stories of their exploits and descriptions of their appearances began to profilerate and helped to undermine their credibility still further. As Professor Tolkien pointed out in *Tree and Leaf* (1964), his study of the fairy story, 'Faërie cannot be caught in a net of words; for it is one of its qualities to be indescribable, though not imperceptible.' Nevertheless, speculation on the nature of Fairyland and its inhabitants has continued to fire the imaginations of British writers to this day.

In the beginning, fairy stories were circulated by word of mouth. The earliest survivors have come to us in ballad form, partly because metrical verse is easy to memorise. Among the anonymous early ballads is that of *Thomas the Rhymer*, who was visited by the Queen of Elfland as he lay on Huntlie Bank in Scotland:

> Her shirt was o' the grass-green silk
> Her mantle o' the velvet fyne
> At ilka tett of her horse's mane
> Hung fifty siller bells and nine.

She manifests all the qualities of a real fairy as defined by Tolkien: dignity, pride, beauty and the power to manipulate human beings.

Sometimes, ballads were foreign in origin, such as *The Romance of King Orfeo*; on the poet's admission, it is a 'Breton lay', such as were popularised in the time of Marie de France in the early 14th century. The story has its origins in the classical myth of Orpheus and Eurydice, but by this period, Pluto and his followers have been transformed into

Arthur Rackham: *The Widow Whitgift and her Sons.* Original illustration to *The Dymchurch Flit* from *Puck of Pook's Hill* by Rudyard Kipling, 1906. (Victoria and Albert Museum)

Overleaf
John Anster Fitzgerald: *Ariel,* c1858-1868 (Walker Art Gallery, Liverpool)

44

the King of the Fairies and a courtly troop of knights mounted on snow-white steeds:

> Their lovely clothes were milky white
> And never yet there struck my sight
> Beings so excellently bright. . . .

The fairy king who seizes Queen Heurodis so forcibly wears a crown that is made of neither silver nor gold:

> But it was of a precious stone
> And brightly, like the sun, it shone.

Chaucer's contemporary, John Gower, describes an irresistible mortal youth in the *Confessio Amantis*, 'as he were of faierie'. By 1400, however, the hypnotic powers he suggests were already metaphorical. As Chaucer's Wife of Bath explains at the opening of her contribution to *The Canterbury Tales*:

> In th' olde dayes of Kyng Arthour
> . . . Al was this land fulfild of fayerye.
> The elf-queene, with hir joly compaignye
> Daunced ful ofte in many a grene mede.
> This was the olde opinion, as I rede;
> I speke of manye hundred yeres ago.
> But now kan no man se none elves mo. . . .

King Arthur—a key figure in early fairy literature—and his court were closely associated with fairies such as the

49

Lady of the Lake and the king's own sister, Morgan le Fay. There is little doubt of the powers of that treacherous lady or those of Nimuë, the fairy who bewitched the magician Merlin. Sir Thomas Malory's *Morte D'Arthur* was first published by Caxton in 1485 and was largely dependent on French sources, as was *Huon of Burdeux*, an extremely influential romance which was translated by Lord Berners and printed by Wynkyn de Worde in about 1534. King Arthur also appears in *Huon of Burdeux*, together with Morgan le Fay, who is said to have married Julius Caesar by whom she had a son, Oberon, the most famous of the fairy kings. Oberon plays a major role in the tale, as patron and bene-

La bonne femme racontant l'histoire de Tom Pouce.

Frontispiece to *Tom Pouce ou Le Petit Garçon,* translated from the English into French by Théodore-Pierre Bertin, 1821. (Ronald Horton)

factor of Huon, and is described, 'of heyght but of iii fote and crokyd shulderyd, but yet he hath an aungelyke vysage. . . .' This is one of the first instances in literature where a fairy, and notably the fairy king, is described as being considerably smaller than adult size. But in spite of his rather unprepossessing appearance as a hunch-backed dwarf, Oberon conducts himself with wisdom and dignity, presents Huon with his bride, Escleremond, and names him heir to fairyland.

Shakespeare is known to have used *Huon of Burdeux* as a source for *A Midsummer Night's Dream*, perhaps the most potent evocation of fairyland ever achieved. Although it is the first play in which the fairy theme is extensively treated, it is by no means the first appearance of fairies in English drama. They participate in the plays of Robert Greene and George Peele, notably *Friar Bacon and Friar Bungay* and *James IV*, which were performed in the late 1580s, and more important in *Endimion*, published in 1591 and written by John Lyly, to whom Shakespeare was indebted.

John Absalon: illustration to *Popular Nursery Tales including Tom Thumb, c*1860. (Ronald Horton)

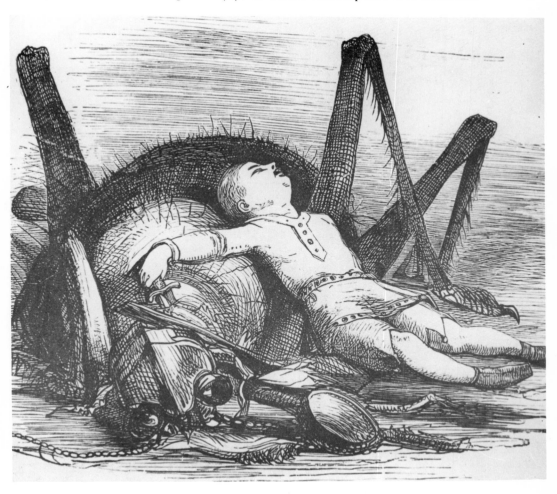

References are made to fairies in several of Shakespeare's plays, particularly as evil spirits of darkness, and associated with changelings. But the first full-length description of a fairy is given by Mercutio in his famous Queen Mab speech in *Romeo and Juliet*, which was probably written in 1595. In a brilliantly sustained evocation, he describes how Mab, the fairies' midwife, comes

> In shape no bigger than an agate-stone
> On the forefinger of an alderman,
> Drawn with a team of little atomies
> Athwart mens' noses as they lie asleep.

and inspires their dreams. Mercutio conjures up a magical vision of the Queen, as small and as delicate as an insect:

> Her waggon-spokes made of long spinners' legs;
> The cover of the wings of grasshoppers. . . .
> Her waggoner, a small grey-coated gnat. . . .
> Her chariot is an empty hazel-nut
> Made by the joiner squirrel or old grub. . . .

His description of the transport of the Fairy Queen was to serve as a model for poets throughout the 17th century, and set the pattern for the diminutive fairy which has lasted to the present day.

The fairies who appear in *A Midsummer Night's Dream* are also conceived as tiny airy beings. They share Queen

Kenny Meadows: illustration to *A Midsummer Night's Dream*, 1852. (Raymond Watkinson)

John Simmons: *Titania* (Private collection, Maas Gallery photograph)

Mab's role as a fertility spirit in blessing the marriages that are celebrated during the course of the play. *The Dream* was probably first performed as a wedding masque in 1595–96, when the fairies may have been played by brides-maids or boys of the household. Their minute size is emphasised throughout the play:

> . . . all their elves for fear
> Creep into acorn-cups, and hide them there.

It is implied that a snake skin is 'Weed wide enough to wrap a fairy in', and Titania imperiously commands her tiny servants to perform tasks suited to their size. She

Richard Doyle: illustration to John Ruskin's *The King of the Golden River*, 1904. (Ronald Horton)

53

instructs some to kill the pests that live in rose buds, some to slay bats for their wings, 'To make my small elves coats', to light tapers from the hairs on the thighs of bumble-bees, and to pluck the wings from butterflies to use as fans. Bottom requests that Cobweb 'kill me a red-hipped humble-bee on the top of a thistle . . . and bring me the honey bag . . . have a care the honey-bag break not; I would be loth to have you overflowen with a honey-bag'.

Descriptions of these tasks of miniature husbandry, together with the bewitching evocations of the countryside uttered by Titania—

> . . . since the middle summer's spring
> Met we on hill, in dale, forest or mead
> By paved fountain or by rushy brook
> Or on the beached margent of the sea
> To dance our ringlets of the whistling wind. . . .

—and by Oberon:

> I know a bank where the wild thyme blows
> Where oxlips and the nodding violet grows
> Quite overcanopied with luscious woodbine,
> With musk-roses and with eglantine. . . .

—remind us that Fairyland is the idealised England of Queen Elizabeth, Spenser's *Faerie Queen*. This work, which is written in the form of a complex allegory, cannot be considered as fairy literature; the latter is distinguished by its independence from the real world, for which it may not stand as a symbol.

An altogether different type of sprite is represented by Puck or Robin Goodfellow, Oberon's henchman. Puck was a hob goblin whose pranks were well known among country folk and were elaborated at length by Reginald Scot, in *The Discoverie of Witchcraft*, first published in 1584. Puck was

Kenny Meadows: illustration to *A Midsummer Night's Dream*, 1852. (Raymond Watkinson)

mischievous and capricious, equally capable of helping or
hindering the householder or maid-servant, and skilled at
'illusion and knaverie'. At his first entry in *The Dream*, a
fairy alludes to his exploits,

> . . . are you not he
> That frights the maidens of the villagery;
> Skim milk, and sometimes labour in the quern,
> And bootless make the breathless housewife churn
> . . .
> Mislead night-wanderers, laughing at their harm?
> Those that Hobgoblin call you, and sweet Puck,
> You do their work, and they shall have good luck.

Puck himself makes reference to his shape-shifting powers.
To the consternation of his victims, he pretends to be a
crab-apple in a bowl of punch, and a three-legged stool.
Later in the play, he prepares to confuse the rustic players
by chasing them in the guises of a horse, a hound, a hog,

a headless bear and even a fire. His mercurial temperament is well suited to the tasks that Oberon sets him.

A later edition of Scot's *The Discoverie of Witchcraft* also speaks of such fairies as Puck, 'jocund and facetious spirits' who are said to '... sport themselves in the night by tumbling and fooling with Servants and shepherds in Country houses, pinching them black and blew. . . .' Such fairies cause considerable discomfort to another of Shakespeare's characters, namely Sir John Falstaff in *The Merry Wives of Windsor*, which was probably written around 1600. On this occasion, however, the fairy identities have been assumed by Mistress Page and her fellow conspirators, to punish Falstaff for his lechery. They arrive at their appointed hour and dance about Herne's Oak until they are further instructed,

> '. . . those that sleep and think not on their sins
> Pinch them, arms, legs, backs, shoulders, sides and shins.'

They then proceed to burn Falstaff with their tapers and to pinch him mercilessly, recalling a very similar scene in Lyly's *Endimion*, in which the unfortunate Corsites suffers such treatment for inadvertent spying and is pinched black and blue.

The last of Shakespeare's plays to include spirit partici-

Illustration to Ludwig Bechstein's *Neues Deutsches Märchenbuch*, c1880. (Ronald Horton)

pants is *The Tempest*, which was completed between 1610 and 1612. During its course, the magician, Prospero, speaks of the elves of

' . . . hills, brooks, standing lakes and groves;
And ye that on the sands with printless foot
Do chase the ebbing Neptune. . . .'

He alludes to those who make the 'green, sour ringlets' (fairy rings) in the grass. But in the play itself, Shakespeare has moved away from the fairies of folklore and has created, in the character of Ariel, an even more elusive sylph, a personification of the air itself. In defining Ariel, who closely resembles a 'sylph', the elemental personification of the air, Shakespeare is surely indebted to the writings of Paracelsus. Ariel is held in thrall by Prospero, for whom he performs such tasks as Puck executed for Oberon, in return for his freedom. At Prospero's command he conjures up a storm in which he portrays lightning:

. . . sometimes I divide
And burn in many places; on the topmast
The yard and boresprit, would I flame distinctly.

He has the capacity to move with amazing speed:

. . . I drink the air before me, and return
Or e'er your pulse twice beat

and thus eclipses even Puck's impressive claim to be able to engirdle the earth in forty minutes. Having achieved such a degree of refinement in his art, after the release of Ariel, Prospero—like Shakespeare himself—consciously decides to lay aside his wand and cease his enchantments.

The 17th century was marked by opposing trends in man's attitude to the supernatural. On one hand, it brought a morbid return to superstition, in the form of the notorious witch-hunts and trials. They were initiated by King James himself, who led the attack on witches and their spirit familiars in his work on *Daemonologie* of 1597, in which he put forward the view that, 'The Phairie . . . was one of the sortes of illusion that was rifest in the time of Papistrie.' Throughout the British Isles, anyone who admitted knowledge of the pagan spirit world, even to the extent of seeing fairies, was liable to be burned as a witch.

On the other hand, some writers, notably Sir Francis Bacon, began to make real attempts to rationalise systems of thought and first formulated the language of scientific scholarship. Such an attempt to shape all the diversity which confronted him into a consistent and viable point of view was made by Robert Burton in *The Anatomy of Melancholy* of 1621. The result, however, was a sprawling and somewhat chaotic composition, displaying varying degrees of interest in the aspects of its subject matter.

Robert Huskisson: *There Sleeps Titania,* 1847. (Private collection, Maas Gallery photograph)

One area in which we have evidence of Burton's interest is that of fairies. Books and manuscripts from his collection are housed in the Bodleian Library, and among them are several unique items connected with fairies, including *A Description of the King and Queene of Fayries* of 1635 and *Tom Thumbe, His Life and Death* of 1630. Burton also devoted a long and fascinating 'Digression on the nature of Spirits, Bad Angels or Divels' in his *Anatomy of Melancholy.* He examines the fairies of British folklore, listed rather indiscriminately under Paracelsus' elemental headings. He speaks of earth spirits as follows: 'Terrestrial divels are those lares, genii, faunes, satyrs, wood-nymphs, foliots, fayries, Robin Goodfellows, Trulli etc. which as they are the most conversant with men, so they do them most harm. . . .'

Burton suggests that some writers equate them with gods of Babylon, Ancient Egypt, Greece and Rome. 'Our fayries,' he continues, 'have been in former times adored with much superstition, with sweeping their houses. . . . These are they that dance on heaths and greens . . . and leave that green circle, which we commonly finde in plain fields, which others hold to proceed from a meteor falling, or some accidental rankness of the ground. . . .'

But if rational thought was now about to eliminate the last vestiges of superstitious belief in fairies from the informed mind, it had little effect on the creative imagination. The publication of *A Midsummer Night's Dream* in 1600 prompted an immediate glut of fairy fiction. The anonymous *The Maydes Metamorphosis* published that same year, portrays fairies of a decidedly earthy nature. The third Fay, 'Little Pricke' by name, describes his antics to

Frederick Goodall: *Fairy Scene,* c1846. (Cecil Higgins Art Gallery, Bedford)

their human interlocutor:

> When I feele a girle asleepe
> Underneath her frock I peepe
> There to sport, and there I play
> Then I byte her like a flea. . . .

Then he invites the human to join their dance, with the now familiar proviso that if he refuses, they will pinch him black and blue. Oberon appears, attended by armies of elves in Christopher Middleton's *Chinon of England* in 1597, and is the eponymous hero of Ben Jonson's masque, *Oberon, the Fairy Prince*, published in 1611. Fairies appear in other of Jonson's masques, and in his unfinished pastoral, *The Sad Shepherd*, Puck-hairy plays an important role in protecting his mistress, Maudlin, Witch of Papplewick, from Robin Hood.

In poetry, Robin Goodfellow's activities in the kitchen and dairy are celebrated in *Of Ghoasts and Goblins* by Samuel Rowlands, which appeared in 1613, in his book, *More Knaves Yet? The Knaves of Spades and Diamonds*. The poem mourns his disappearance and replacement by Robin Badfellow.

In the second song of *Britannia's Pastorals*, published between 1613 and 1616, William Browne of Tavistock, and also of the Inner Temple, uses allusions to fairies to set his rural scene describing their dances,

> Which in the meadow made such circles greene,
> As if with garlands it had crowned beene. . . .

And he elaborates on the Fairy Queen's moral attitude to housewifery.

One of the most famous fairy poems of this period is *Nimphidia, the Court of Fayrie* by Michael Drayton, which was published, together with *The Bataille of Agincourt*, in 1627. Drayton was a good friend of William Browne, in whose preface to *Britannia's Pastorals* he wrote a dedication. Drayton also moved in the same circles as William Burton, brother of Robert; and together with John Donne, Ben Jonson and Robert Herrick, he enjoyed the enlightened patronage of Edward Sackville, 2nd Earl of Dorset, at whose country seat, Knole in Kent, they were all accustomed to meet. On such occasions, they may well have stimulated one another in writing fairy pieces. *Nimphidia* is a burlesque, loosely based on Arthurian romance, and concerns the illicit love of the Fairy Knight, Pigwiggen, for Oberon's Queen Mab. In jaunty rhyme the story is unfolded of the lovers' tryst, Oberon's jealousy and pursuit, the tricking of Puck by the Fairy Nimphidia, the combat between Pigwiggen and Oberon and their eventual reconciliation through the ministrations of Proserpina, Queen

Mab's ally. There are the accustomed references to fairy tasks undertaken on behalf of mortals, to Mab as the begetter of dreams and nightmares, and to changelings. The description of Mab's chariot is based on Mercutio's Queen Mab speech. Oberon's encounters with various insects during his search for his Queen border on the ridiculous. The most memorable passage concerns Pigwiggen as he prepares to face Oberon in battle:

> And quickly armes him for the Field:
> A little Cockle-shell his shield. . . . ,
> And puts him on a Coate of Male,
> Which was of a Fishe's scale. . . ,
> His Rapier was a Hornet's sting,
> It was a very dangerous thing. . . ,
> His Helmet was a Beetle's head,
> Most horrible and full of dread. . . ,
> Himselfe he on an Earewig set,
> Yet scarce he on his back could get. . . .

Robert Herrick wrote a series of fairy poems which were published in the *Hesperides* in 1648. In common with much 17th century poetry, they are spun out of conceits connected with minuteness. *The Fairies* is a short, brisk poem which issues the usual warning to those who do not keep their houses in order, for 'sluts are loathesome to the fairie.' Then follow three linked poems, *The Fair Temple: or Oberon's Chapel*, *Oberon's Diet*, and *Oberon's Palace*. The imagery of *The Temple* is exceedingly complex, for not only are there detailed descriptions given of the building and its services, on a consistently miniature scale, but a mild satire on Catholic ritual is also implied. The structure is described both as a classical temple and as a Catholic cathedral, since

> Theirs is a mixed religion
> And some have heard the elves it call
> Part Pagan, part Papistical. . . .

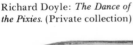

Richard Doyle: *The Dance of the Pixies.* (Private collection)

There is also mention of the 'mumbling mass-priest' and

the possibility of the election of Elve Boniface to the Papacy. Statues of insects as idols stand side by side with saints Tit, Nit, Is and Itis. A nutshell serves as a font, the altar cloth is made of a codling skin fringed with a spangle-work of dew, the copes and surplices are made of cobweb and a dried apple core is rung for matins and evensong.

After his observances, Oberon proceeds to the feast that has been prepared for him. He first whets his appetite with

> A pure seed-pearl of infant dew
> Bought and besweetened in a blue
> And pregnant violet. . . .

He follows with a number of mouth-watering courses:

> . . . the sagg
> And wee bestrutted bee's sweet bag;
> Gladding his palate with some store
> Of emmets' eggs; what would he more,
> But beards of mice, a newt's stewed thigh
> A bloated earwig and a fly. . . .

Gorged and slightly tipsy he proceeds, in *Oberon's Palace*, to join Queen Mab in the bedchamber in a magical and

Beauty entertained with Invisible Music.

Anon: illustration to *Beauty and the Beast* (attributed to Charles and Mary Lamb). (Ronald Horton)

The Pumpkin, and the Rat, and the Mice, and the Lizards, being changed by the Fairy, into a
Coach, Horses, and Servants, to take Cinderella to the Ball at the Royal Palace

The Fairy changing Cinderella's Kitchen dress. into a. beautiful Ball dress

erotic evocation. It is hung with snake skins and the eyes
from peacocks' tails and lit by glow-worms' eyes and the
reflections from fish-scales. Mab herself lies on a bed of
dandelions, wrapped in sheets made of a membraneous
caul behind a curtain of cobweb hung with tears

> Dropt from the eyes of ravished girls
> Or writhing brides. . . .

The bedchamber of the Fairy King and Queen is conceived
as the embodiment of sexual fantasy, for in Fairyland can
be realised the wildest and most pagan dreams.

A lesser writer, but one whose work is of considerable
interest, was Margaret Cavendish, Duchess of Newcastle.
Her *Poems and Fancies,* published in 1653, shows a marked
dependence on Shakespeare, Drayton and Herrick. She
wrote a number of fairy poems; some are concerned with
the daily life of Queen Mab, perhaps in answer to Herrick's
Oberon and largely derived from him. They include *The*

Pastime and Recreation of the Queen of the Fairies in Fairyland, the Centre of the Earth where Mab dines from a mushroom table spread with a cobweb and feasts on ' . . . Amelets made of Ants-eggs new. . . . Her milk comes from the Dormouse udder' In *Her Descending Downe* she retires to her chamber whose hangings are of rainbows:

> Her bed a cherry-stone carved throughout
> And with a Butter-flyes wing hung about
> Her sheets are made of a Doves eye skin
> Her pillow a Violet bud laid therein.

Margaret Cavendish includes *A Battle between King Oberon and the Pygmees*, largely drawn from Drayton, but her most characteristic poems concern the fairies seen literally as 'atomies' within the brain. She speculates on fairies and their effects on our thoughts:

> Who knows, but in the Braine may dwel
> Little small Fairies, who can tell?. . .
> And the place where memory doth lye in
> Is the great magazine of Oberon King.

John Milton refers to fairies in two very lively passages, both with their origins in folk tradition rather than in earlier literature. In *L'Allegro*, written in the 1630s, he evokes wonderfully the fireside exchange of fairy stories:

> Stories told of many a feat
> How Faery Mab the junkets eat
> She was pincht and pull'd she sed,
> And he by Friar's Lanthorn led. . . .

And in the first book of *Paradise Lost*, completed in the 1660s, he takes a telescopic view of the fallen angels as they build Pandaemonium, likening them to

> . . . . Faëry elves
> whose midnight revels by a forest side
> Or fountain, some belated peasant sees,
> Or dreams he sees while overhead the Moon
> Sits arbitress. . . .

There has always been a certain amount of dispute over the immortality of fairies. Burton had held them to be mortal, though devils. Ritson, the compiler of fairy tales, firmly believed the opposite: 'The Fairies never died, a position of which there is every kind of proof that a fact can require.'

One thing men of literature did agree on was that, by the late 17th century, many fairies had left England. Perhaps it was a sign of growing literary rationality. Rowlands had earlier alluded to the departure of Robin Goodfellow.

65

Bishop Corbet, whose *Certain Elegant Poems* of 1647 contained *A Proper New Ballad: The Fairies Farewell*, mourned their passing and the loss of fairy assistance with household drudgery. Some mementoes remained:

> Witness those rings and roundelays
> Of theirs which yet remain
> Were footed in Queen Mary's days
> On many a grassy plain
> But since of late Elizabeth
> And later James came in
> They never danced on any heath
> As when the time hath bin.

He concluded that they must either have died or fled abroad, possibly for religious reasons. There was much sighing for the Golden Age of Albion when the country was 'fulfild of fayerye'. John Selden shakes his head in his *Table Talk*, and swears, 'There never was a merry world since the fairies left dancing and the parson left conjuring.' The German writer Schiller expressed this poignant regret admirably in his play, *Wallenstein*, which was translated by Coleridge:

> The old fable-existences are no more
> The fascinating race has emigrated
> . . . The fair humanities of old religions
> That had their haunt in dale or piny mountain
> . . . Or chasms and watery depths,—all these have vanished
> They live no longer in the age of reason. . . .

Curiously enough, Alexander Pope, one of the most rational of the Augustan poets, was probably responsible for the creation of the first winged fairies in English literature. In *The Rape of the Lock*, he describes the creatures he terms elemental 'sylphs'. Dr Katharine Briggs, who is better qualified than most to judge, suggests in *Fairies in Tradition and Literature* (1967) that they are actually fairies. Pope's language does bear out this point of view:

> Some to the Sun their Insect-Wings unfold,
> Waft on the Breeze, or sink in clouds of Gold
> . . . Loose to the Wind their airy Garments flew
> Thin glitt'ring Textures of the filmy Dew. . .
> Dipt in the richest Tincture of the Skies
> Where Light disports in ever-mingling Dies. . .

The English Romantic poets remained surprisingly uninterested in fairy lore. Perhaps they preferred to mourn with Schiller and Coleridge for the lost gods. Shelley's *Queen Mab* is an abstraction wrapped in clouds from which emanates a 'purpureal halo'. In *La Belle Dame Sans Merci*, however, Keats creates a fairy being of lasting potency, a damsel of fatal beauty cast in the medieval mould:

> I met a lady in the meads
> Full beautiful, a faery's child
> Her hair was long, her foot was light
> And her eyes were wild.

The advent of the fairy-tale collectors in the 17th century may well have helped to hasten the end of widespread popular belief in fairies in the British Isles. For a while the fairies of British folk legend were all but vanquished by an invasion of foreign stories and imported *fées*. The earliest anthology of fairy tales was compiled by an Italian, Giovanni Straparola in 1550, and contained the story of *Puss in Boots*. In the late 17th century, the fashion arose for making collections of courtly fairy stories, which were originally told to the children of the French nobility and compiled by such as the Comtesse D'Aulnoy, the Perraults father and son, Mme de Murat and Mme de Villeneuve—who published *Beauty and the Beast*.

All these were available in English translations in the early 18th century at which time the Fairy Godmother was introduced into the personae of Fairyland and quickly gained the ascendancy. The purpose of fairy stories changed correspondingly; since the imported fairies made human morals their chief concern, the accounts of their deeds and homilies were held to be improving for the character and therefore eminently suitable reading matter for children. For many years, the British child endured the rap of the fairy wand across the knuckles, and it was not until the early 19th century that children's literature was freed, albeit temporarily, from the bondage of moral instruction, and fairy stories were again read seriously by adults.

The first English edition of *German Popular Stories*, compiled by the German brothers Grimm, appeared in 1823, and works, largely of his own invention, by Hans Andersen, that other great foreign writer of fairy tales, were being translated by 1850. For a while, interest in indigenous folk tales was all but eclipsed. In 1825, however, Crofton Croker published his *Fairy Tales of the South of Ireland*; this was followed in 1831 by Joseph Ritson's *Fairy Tales* and in 1836 by Mrs Bray's *Traditions of the Borders of the Tamar and Tavy*. There followed a stream of anthologies and critical histories of British folk and fairy stories. Most famous among children's anthologies were the twelve coloured fairy books of Andrew Lang, the first of which appeared in 1889. At the same time, ballads were being collected and interpreted by creative writers such as Sir Walter Scott, whose *Minstrelsy of the Scottish Border* appeared in 1801. Thomas Moore published his *Irish Melodies* in 1845, F. J. Child his *English and Scottish Popular Ballads* in 1882 and W. B. Yeats his *Irish Fairy and Folk Tales* in 1888. These volumes contained the definitive versions of many of the best known fairy ballads.

There are references to fairies scattered throughout Scott's own poems. They are not his best work but are nevertheless lively and steeped in fairy traditions of the Borders. After him, writers of fairy literature tended to fall into different camps. There were a number of hack writers who continued to produce mawkish tales and whimsical poems cast in traditional moulds. There were those who produced startlingly original stories on well established themes. And there were others who adopted traditional themes with an ulterior moral motive.

William Roscoe, M.P. for Liverpool, produced the first children's fantasy without an improving purpose. *The Butterfly's Ball and The Grasshopper's Feast* was published in 1807 and its particular conceit in anthropomorphising insects

William Thackeray: *The Fairy Blackstick,* illustration to the author's *The Rose and the Ring,* 1855. (Raymond Watkinson)

and plants had many imitators. Moralists still abounded, and Cruickshank reinterpreted *Hop o' my Thumb*, *Cinderella* and *Jack and the Beanstalk* as temperance tracts. Dickens replied indignantly to this tampering in *Frauds on the Fairies* from *Household Words* of 1853:

> In a utilitarian age, of all other times, it is a matter of grave importance that Fairy Tales should be respected . . . everyone who has considered the subject knows full well that a nation without fancy, without some romance, never did, never can, never will hold a great place under the sun. . . .

George Macdonald, imbued as he was with the folklore of Aberdeenshire, was also a moralist at heart. In *The Princess and the Goblin* of 1872, the lines are drawn up between the evil goblins of the mines and the angelically beautiful and righteous Fairy Great-Grandmother of the Princess. In Thackeray's *The Rose and the Ring* of 1855, however, the bad-tempered Fairy Blackstick is portrayed as a parody of a Fairy Godmother, who discovers the practical difficulties presented by fairy gifts:

> Fairy roses, fairy rings,
> Turn out sometimes troublesome things.

A group of writers and artists to whom the lure of medieval romance and the idea of a green and pleasant land 'fulfild of fayerye' must have appealed strongly were the Pre-Raphaelite Brotherhood. Even their champion, John Ruskin, abandoned didacticism for once in his story *The King of the Golden River* of 1851. It follows a true folk pattern. Mary de Morgan, whose brother William was closely associated with William Morris, was the author of many ingenious fairy stories. Christina Rossetti created a

Anon: Frontispiece to *Chat in the Playroom and Life at a Farmhouse*, c1870. (Ronald Horton)

most disturbing vision in her portrayal of the malignant goblins in *Goblin Market* in 1852:

> Backward up the mossy glen
> Turned and trooped the goblin men. . . .
> They stood stock still upon the moss
> Leering at each other
> Brother with queer brother
> Signalling each other
> Brother with sly brother.

The Irish writer William Allingham produced a number of vigorous fairy poems such as *The Music Masters*, and *The Maids of Elfinmere*, which were published in 1855, and *In Fairyland*, which was published in 1870 with illustrations by Dicky Doyle. In his most famous poem, Allingham hints at the menace expounded in *Goblin Market*:

> Up the airy mountain
> Down the rushy glen
> We dare not go a-hunting
> For fear of little men. . . .

In the poems of W. B. Yeats we sense a fresh note of strangeness and enchantment. Yeats actually believed in fairies. His was a practical, sincere belief, yet full of vague yearnings that gave such poignancy to the lines:

> Come away, O human child!
> To the woods and waters wild
> With a fairy hand in hand,
> For the world's more full of weeping than you can understand.

More recently, literary fairies have had a rather chequered career. A great number of the late 19th and early 20th century fairy stories lapsed into whimsy and sentimentality, notably in the work of Rose Fyleman and Enid Blyton. Occasionally, writers emerged who had not lost touch with their folk roots and who railed against the degeneration of the tradition, as Kipling did through Puck in *Puck of Pook's Hill* in 1906: 'Besides, what you call *them* are made-up things the People of the Hills have never heard of—little buzzflies with butterfly wings and gauze petticoats. . . . Butterfly wings indeed!'

J. M. Barrie captured much of the essence of Fairyland in a number of his works. The theme of the child whose life is changed irrevocably through contact with Fairyland is dealt with in *Peter Pan*. It is also treated with greater subtlety in *Mary Rose*, about a girl who eventually disappears forever into the Never Never Land.

It is human nature to long for enchantment. Andrew Lang held that fairy stories were designed for children with an 'unblunted edge of belief and a fresh appetite for marvels.' It is not necessary to believe in such things but only to have one's desire aroused. Adults, as Professor Tolkien has noted, have a far greater need of an escape valve from reality than do children, as the enormous success of his own books, *The Hobbit* and *The Lord of the Rings* trilogy has most emphatically proved.

W.R. Ingram: *Ariel on the Bat's Back.* (Editions Graphiques, London)

Theatre

Then come the fairies. Can even genius succeed in putting fairies on the stage? (Harley Granville-Barker)

For centuries, producers have attempted to represent fairies convincingly on the stage. From Shakespeare onwards, there has been a glittering progression of fairies in plays, operas, ballets and pantomimes which reached its peak in the 19th century. This survey of fairies on the stage looks separately at each of these theatrical genres, beginning with a 17th century masque—an entertainment that embraced several different theatrical forms.

A Masque: *Oberon, the Fairy Prince*

The masque was primarily a dance drama, with verse commentary. It was a favourite entertainment in the English Court of the 17th century. The magnificent scenery and costumes for many masques were devised by the artist and architect Inigo Jones.

Oberon, the Fairy Prince was written by Ben Jonson and designed by Jones to honour Henry, Prince of Wales, who, aged 16, took the title role. The masque was performed on 1st January 1611, in the Banqueting House and was attended by James I, his family and foreign ambassadors to his court.

This masque, a stupendous allegory, was a celebration of the English monarchy, from Arthur to James I—seen as the ideal monarch—and Prince Henry, a youth of destiny for both England and Europe. This was magnificently proclaimed by Oberon's 'fays' (fairy knights) and guardian sylvans, by Silenus and his normally recalcitrant satyrs.

The highlight of the masque was its series of sumptuous scenes. As described in the stage directions, the 'whole palace opened, and the nation of fays were discovered, some with instruments, some bearing lights, others singing . . . Oberon, in a chariot . . . to a loud triumphant music began to move forward, drawn by two white bears . . . guarded by three sylvans.'

The single performance cost over £2,000. Performers danced together and with the audience to the music of violins, hautboys, lutes and cornets. A spectator, William Trumbull the elder, described the costumes: '. . . then came the gentlemen in short scarlet hose and white brodequins full of silver spangles coming halfway to the calf . . . some wearing jackets with white folds as the Roman emperors . . . all in gold and silver cloth, white and scarlet feathers on their heads and very high white plumes . . .' Inigo Jones's elaborate and inventive designs have proved a rich source of inspiration to later artists.

Inigo Jones: *Oberon, The Fairy Prince,* costume design, 1611. (The Courtauld Institute of Art and the Devonshire Collection, Trustees of the Chatsworth Collection)

SHAKESPEARE

The most celebrated fairies of the English stage are those created by Shakespeare. Immortal characters from immortal plays, who have fascinated and challenged generations of producers and actors, they have been subject to widely differing interpretations and fashions.

The stories are familiar. *A Midsummer Night's Dream*, written about 1594, has fairies who come out at midnight and hasten away at sunrise. Oberon derives from the King of the Fairies in the romance of *Huon of Burdeux*. Titania, their queen, is probably based on Diana in Ovid's *Metamorphoses*. They are attended by trains of tiny elves and fairies. Puck, their chief messenger, is based on Robin Goodfellow, hobgoblin of English folklore. David Young describes these fairies as 'a curious mixture of woodspirits and household gods, pagan deities and local pixies . . . Through Titania and her train, Shakespeare emphasises their innocence and delicacy; in Oberon and Puck, he expresses their darker side, potentially malevolent in the lore of the time.'

The Tempest was written in about 1611. Ariel, the airy spirit—a mixture of many elements, including English folklore, magical tradition and classical mythology—can create tempests, take on any form, become invisible. Throughout the play, he is employed by Prospero to carry out his designs. Ariel's answer to Prospero's summons describes his role:

> All hail, great master! grave sir, hail! I come
> To answer thy best pleasure: be't to fly,
> To swim, to dive into the fire, to ride
> On the curl'd clouds, to thy strong bidding task
> Ariel and all his quality. (I,ii, 189–193)

Up to the 19th century, few visual records exist of the fairies from either play in performance, and from the 17th century until well into the 19th century both plays were performed with distorted texts. *A Midsummer Night's Dream*, in particular, was produced in 'operatised' or bowdlerised versions; an additional sub-plot was added to *The Tempest*. But since the restoration of the original texts, many distinguished productions have represented these fairies in widely different and imaginative ways. Some of the more noteworthy presentations are recalled below.

William Macready (1793–1873): *The Tempest*, The Theatre Royal, Covent Garden, 1838
'Could not recover myself from the excitement of last night. The scenes of the storm, the flights of Ariel, and the enthusiasm of the house were constantly recurring to me.' So read the entry in William Macready's diary for 14th

October 1838. His production of *The Tempest*, a bold venture which rescued Shakespeare from the adapters, presenting the text in large part restored, had opened at Covent Garden the previous night. Macready, whose aim was to produce Shakespeare with a new magnificence and appropriateness of scenery and costume, had agonized over every detail. He was almost universally acclaimed by the audiences and the press. But it was his 'gentle' Ariel, played by Miss Priscilla Horton, who really stole the show. She had spent the previous September learning to fly on wires, and sang to a delighted audience while suspended in mid-air.

Miss Priscilla Horton as Ariel, *The Tempest*, The Theatre Royal Covent Garden, 1838. (Theatre Museum, Victoria and Albert Museum)

Madame Vestris (1797–1856): *A Midsummer Night's Dream*,
The Theatre Royal, Covent Garden, 1840

In 1840, again at Covent Garden, *A Midsummer Night's Dream* was produced, almost as written by Shakespeare, for the first time since 1642. Madame Vestris's lavish revival conjured up fairyland by means of the latest theatrical devices: gauzes, indirect lighting, movable and gliding panoramic scenery.

An excited spectator, the correspondent 'E. R. W.' in *The Theatrical Journal*, described the scene in a wood near Athens. There was a lake hemmed round with trees, a star-bespangled sky, a pale moon pouring down her silvery light: '. . . mischevious Puck shoots up from the earth, other spirits come—the mighty Oberon, Titania, and all her beauteous court, till so life-like all becomes, that we are in fairyland . . . Puck flies away, Oberon waving his wand, melts the scene from our sight, and leaves a forest glade . . .' The part of Oberon was played by no less a lady than Madame herself, a convention of the time.

In the final scene, great pains were taken to illustrate Shakespeare's text precisely. At Oberon's command, the stage was filled with fairies 'clad in virgin white and immaculate silk stockings', carrying twinkling coloured lights, flitting and dancing through the house. The play was accompanied, for the first time, by the strains of Mendelssohn. In all, it was a production that must have satisfied 'the most fastidious voluptuary in scenic art', pronounced *John Bull*.

Madame Vestris as Oberon, *A Midsummer Night's Dream,* The Theatre Royal Covent Garden, 1840. (Theatre Museum, Victoria and Albert Museum)

Charles Kean (1811–68): *A Midsummer Night's Dream*, The Princess's Theatre, 1856

Charles Kean continued, with further embellishments, the tradition of scenic splendour inherited from his predecessors. For his productions, Shakespeare's texts of *A Midsummer Night's Dream* and *The Tempest* were greatly reduced with the loss of much poetry. Elaborate scenery, mechanical effects, dancing and music abounded. But although his shows attracted enthusiastic crowds and reviews, some contemporary critics found them less than convincing. *Lloyd's Weekly Newspaper*, reviewing *A Midsummer's Night Dream*, talked of 'Extraneous exhibitions which dazzle the eyes and lull the judgement.'

A Midsummer Night's Dream, which ran for one hundred and fifty nights, was Kean's prettiest success. The immortals inhabited a wood of beautiful changing scenes and shifting dioramas, first moonlit then in rising sunlight with dissolving mists. Finally, in Theseus' splendid palace, fairies 'glittering in the most brilliant dresses, with a crust of bullion about their legs, cause the curtain to fall on a splendid ballet' wrote Henry Morley, who continued, 'and it is evidence enough of the depraved taste of the audience to say that the ballet is encored.'

Ellen Terry, a precocious eight-year-old, took the part of Puck. Puck's opening speech in Act II was given to a fairy, while Miss Terry entered, rising on a mechanical

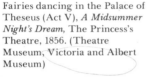

Fairies dancing in the Palace of Theseus (Act V), *A Midsummer Night's Dream,* The Princess's Theatre, 1856. (Theatre Museum, Victoria and Albert Museum)

mushroom to the playing of sweet music. In such a long run, there were the inevitable mishaps. When Puck was told to put a girdle round the earth in forty minutes, she ran from the stage as fast as possible, and a dummy Puck was hurled through the air from the point where she had disappeared. One night, the dummy fell on the stage and, concerned for its safety, Miss Terry ran on, picked it up and ran off to roars of laughter. Another night, she had almost come up through a trap to give her final speech, but a man shut the trap door too soon and caught her toe, causing her great pain. After some commotion, Mrs Kean rushed on to the stage and promised her double pay if she would finish the performance. She did, and earned thirty shillings that night.

The eight-year-old Ellen Terry seated on a mechanical mushroom, *A Midsummer Night's Dream*, 1856. (The National Trust, Ellen Terry Memorial Museum)

Charles Kean (1811–68): *The Tempest*, The Princess's Theatre, 1857

July 1857 saw Kean's production of *The Tempest*. In the preface to his acting edition, he implored the indulgence of the public should there be any lengthened delays between the acts of the early performances, as 'scenic appliances are of a more expensive and complicated nature than have ever yet been attempted in any theatre in Europe.'

The mechanical effects and scene changes were astounding throughout a performance pervaded by music from an invisible choir. Ariel, played by Kate Terry, sailed over smooth waters on a dolphin's back, rode on a bat, floated across the sands. At the end of the play, Prospero's spirits were released and flew through the air from the island. Morning broke; Prospero spoke the Epilogue from the deck of the ship which gradually sailed away, bound for Naples. The island receded and Ariel, who was on the bowsprit, now remained alone, liberated, floating in mid-air, watching the departure of his former master to the sounds of the distant chorus of spirits.

Herbert Beerbohm Tree (1853–1917): *A Midsummer Night's Dream*, Her Majesty's Theatre, 1900

The final dress rehearsal for Beerbohm Tree's *A Midsummer Night's Dream* of 1900 was a fiasco. 'The poor, tired little fairies had all been sent home at midnight, stuffed with

Miss Julia Neilson as Oberon,
A Midsummer Night's Dream,
Her Majesty's Theatre, 1900.
(Mander and Mitchenson)

Left
The Tempest, Last Scene, The Princess's Theatre, 1857. Engraving from the *Illustrated London Evening News,* 18th July 1857. (East Sussex County Library, Hove Central Library)

79

sandwiches and stuffed into cabs,' recalled Mrs Tree. The leading members of the cast remained to discuss how to avert a disaster. Their discussion bore fruit. The first night was one of Beerbohm Tree's greatest triumphs with 'fairies, lighting and scenery as had never been seen before'.

The joyful fairies, wearing the colours of nature, green or brown silk or flower petals, appeared from behind bulrushes or shrubs. They revelled in the wood inhabited by singing birds, live rabbits and glow worms; they danced among the pillars of Theseus' palace, which was illuminated by a mysterious (electric) light. Miss Julia Neilson, whose dignified, imposing Oberon made her the star of the play, was dressed in golden, flowing robes with an electric coronal and breastplate and Mrs Tree, a graceful Titania, wore delicately shaded tulle and flowers in her hair.

Mendelssohn's score was presented in its entirety, necessitating a 'somewhat slow and elocutionary delivery' of some of Shakespeare's passages, as the critic from the *Illustrated London News* remarked. But music lovers flocked to the play to hear, uninterrupted, the beautifully played overture.

Harley Granville-Barker (1877–1946): *A Midsummer Night's Dream*, The Savoy Theatre, 1914

Harley Granville-Barker considered that the fairies are the test of the producer. It was assured that they would sound beautiful: verse was Shakespeare's natural medium and first love. But how should they look? Barker and Norman Wilkinson, who designed the costumes, arrived at an almost revolutionary solution for the production at the Savoy in 1914. All the immortals, except Puck—who wore scarlet, with berries in his hair—were presented as golden figures with 'gold hair, gold faces, gold to the tips of their toes' and 'looking like Cambodian idols' in the words of the critic from *The Times*. There were only four golden children: Peasblossom, Cobweb, Moth and Mustardseed. Adults played the other fairies.

At first encounter, the fairies were startling, but on seeing the play a second time, Desmond McCarthy, reviewing for the *New Statesman*, noted that they 'group themselves motionless about the stage, and the lovers move past and between them as casually as though they were stocks or stones. It is without effort we believe these quaintly gorgeous, metallic creatures are invisible to human eyes.'

Clarity, simplicity and greater authenticity were keynotes in Barker's production. His methods of staging were revolutionary in England. Naturalistic settings were rejected and only two scenes were used, the Wood near Athens, and the Palace of Theseus. These were evoked

Loudon Sainthill: *A Sea Creature*, costume design for *The Tempest*, Shakespeare Memorial Theatre, Stratford upon Avon, 1952. (Harry Tatlock Miller)

Overleaf
Francis Danby: *Scene from A Midsummer Night's Dream*, 1832. (Oldham Art Gallery and Museum)

with economy. He presented the text unabridged, spoken at a livelier, more natural tempo than was customary in performances of this play.

Cecil Sharp, who arranged and composed the music, banished all memory of Mendelssohn. For this essentially English play, he substituted English folk tunes and music derived from them. The dances, too, were adapted from English folk dances. Sharp claimed that elements such as these could help the action of the play, whereas Mendelssohn distorted the meaning of the songs, the words becoming mere pegs on which the music was hung.

Basil Dean (1888–1978): *A Midsummer Night's Dream*, The Theatre Royal, Drury Lane, 1924
Basil Dean had only five weeks in which to prepare this production. When it opened on 27th December 1924, the performance was hailed as a grandiose panorama of scene and colour and music. It was the last in the line of lavish Tree-style productions.

Puck and a Fairy, *A Midsummer Night's Dream,* The Savoy Theatre, 1914. (Theatre Museum, Victoria and Albert Museum)

Edmund Dulac: She found herself face to face with a stately and beautiful lady, original drawing for *Beauty and the Beast,* 1910. (Victoria and Albert Museum)

The play included much ballet. Michael Fokine, the famous Russian dancer and choreographer, had trained the fairies. The disused practice room at the theatre was reopened for rehearsals. By order of the Board of Education, a schoolmistress waited in the wings to ensure that those fairies who were under fourteen years of age continued with their studies when they were not rehearsing.

In this production, Puck, played by Mr B. Hay-Petrie, was given a satyr's ears which *The Stage* considered to be novel, but not properly belonging to *A Midsummer Night's Dream*. This ugly figure, with a peering, oldish face, on a dirty, hairy, twisted body contrasted with the glittering, immaculate little fairies and nymphs who seemed to have come straight from the modiste.

Tyrone Guthrie (1900–71): *A Midsummer Night's Dream*, The Old Vic Theatre, 1937

Guthrie, Mendelssohn, Messel and de Valois joined forces with Shakespeare in a presentation of *A Midsummer Night's Dream* that opened at the Old Vic on Boxing Day afternoon, 1937. 'White muslin, pink roses, silver crowns, moonlight and wings . . . These *are* fairies,' declared *The Times* the following day.

This Christmas event was enjoyed by hundreds of children. Tyrone Guthrie recorded that the Queen took the young Princesses Elizabeth and Margaret. The heir to the throne nearly lost her life. She was so intrigued by the fairies and so determined to see how they flew that she was finally hanging out of the Royal Box, held by her feet!

Michael Fokine rehearsing the fairy ballets for *A Midsummer Night's Dream*, The Theatre Royal, Drury Lane, 1924. Double page spread from the *Illustrated London News*, 27th December 1924. (East Sussex County Library, Hove Central Library)

Vivien Leigh as Titania, Ralph Richardson as Bottom and Robert Helpmann as Oberon in *A Midsummer Night's Dream,* The Old Vic Theatre, 1937. (Mander and Mitchenson)

The flying ballets, which were performed by ballet students, had been composed by Ninette de Valois in the 19th century Romantic style. According to the producer, this was *A Midsummer Night's Dream* in the Early Victorian manner.

Oliver Messel had designed the costumes and sets. The curtain rose to reveal black boughs and glittering fairies silhouetted against a gigantic moon. Giant flowers, painted on gauze screens, reduced the fairies to tiny dimensions.

The beautiful Vivien Leigh, as Titania, was a graceful fairy queen. But the outstanding performance was given by the dancer Robert Helpmann as Oberon. A shimmering figure with a pallid visage, sequined eyelids and antlered head-dress, this strange, fantastic creature glided and pirouetted through the wood, his musical voice singing out the verses. This 'Oberon flashes with power, and presides, as Oberons do rarely, over the whole magic of the wood' wrote correspondent of *The Times*.

George Devine (1910–65) **and Marius Goring** (b. 1912):
The Tempest, the Old Vic Theatre, 1940
In 1940, a war-time production of *The Tempest* played for
five weeks at the Old Vic. The producers, the designer
(Oliver Messel) and John Gielgud as Prospero created so
convincing an enchanted isle that one of the actors claimed
that on certain evenings it seemed more real than the whole
war. The decor was necessarily economical: a shimmering,
barren, rocky landscape.

> Come away, servant, Come! I'm ready now.
> Approach, my Ariel; come! (I, ii, 1.187–188)

This was a quivering, darting Ariel, nimble in a silvery
costume, a true servant of a truly magical Prospero, who
never looked at him, seeing him only in the mind.

Marius Goring as Ariel, *The Tempest*, The Old Vic Theatre, 1940. (Vic-Wells Association)

Michael Benthall (1919–74): *The Tempest*, The Royal
Shakespeare Theatre, Stratford upon Avon, 1952

'A flash in the air', wrote the critic from *The Daily Telegraph*;
'a very odd, elongated Ariel, but it does appear to come
from another world' ran the review in *Punch*. Both described
Margaret Leighton's Ariel at Stratford in 1952.

   The performance was designed by Loudon Sainthill,
whose spectacle created a fantasy isle. The very beautiful,
but unconvincing, storm was created by nymphs in filmy
skirts, brandishing scarves. The set showed a mysterious
green light, giant sea shells and jagged rocks. The sea
creatures were imaginative fairy spirits with not a little
hint of Inigo Jones.

Peter Brook (b. 1925): *A Midsummer Night's Dream*, The
Royal Shakespeare Theatre, Stratford upon Avon, 1970
Peter Brook was determined to look at *A Midsummer Night's
Dream* entirely afresh and seek the hidden play behind the
text. In July 1970, Stratford saw his revolutionary
interpretation. The text was intact and very well spoken:
this was Shakespeare seen from an entirely new viewpoint.
As with certain of the other *dramatis personae*, Theseus and
Hippolyta (Alan Howard and Sara Kestelman) doubled
with Oberon and Titania—possibly their dream selves.
The dream world and real world were interwoven.

The production was designed by Sally Jacobs. The set
was a bare, brilliantly lit white room. Ropes and trapezes
dangled from the flies, from which Titania descended in a
bower of ostrich feathers. From a balcony, which ran along
three walls, musicians played music such as had never
previously accompanied this play, on instruments ranging
from guitar to plastic hose; fairies, all but one of them
hearty young men, dangled wires on fishing rods to represent the trees of the Wood near Athens. Whilst swinging
on trapezes, Puck, in yellow pantaloons, tossed a silver
platter—the flower, love in idleness—to Oberon, who spun
it with the expertise of a circus performer.

As in the Elizabethan theatre, the audience became
active participants. With the words of the Epilogue, 'Give
me your hands if we be friends,' Puck, closely followed by
other members of the cast, leapt into the audience and
caught the hands of the nearest spectators.

A scene from Peter Brook's
production of *A Midsummer
Night's Dream*, 1970.
(Shakespeare Birthplace Trust)

Peter Hall (b. 1930): *The Tempest*, The Old Vic Theatre, 1974

This play was the first produced by Peter Hall as director of the National Theatre. It was presented as a masque, spectacular and brilliantly colourful with ample use of stage machinery.

Prospero was played by Gielgud. Michael Feast played an everchanging Ariel who, in the words of Peter Ansorge, writing in *Plays and Players*, 'descends from a bone-like trapeze to ensnare the island visitors in a court of monsters who might have been kidnapped from a Hieronymus Bosch canvas.' Ariel made a spectacular entrance attired in pure white. Now he sang to Ferdinand in counter tenor, now he played a gnashing bird-like harpy, the instrument of Prospero's revenge. An image of Prospero's thought, his powers were finally, suddenly withdrawn, 'marking the running down of Prospero's own tempestuous mind.'

John Gielgud as Prospero, Michael Feast as Ariel in Peter Hall's production of *The Tempest*, The Old Vic Theatre, 1974. (Zoë Dominic)

A Midsummer Night's Dream has not only inspired the dramatic actor and his producer, but also musicians and dancers. It has often been translated into other theatrical forms. Three stage adaptations this century are of particular note.

Constant Lambert (1905–51): *The Fairy Queen*, The Royal Opera House, Covent Garden, 1946
The Fairy Queen, an adaptation of *A Midsummer Night's Dream*, was a spectacular masque, with music by Purcell, which gave equal opportunity to singers, dancers and actors. It was first played at the Dorset Garden Theatre, in 1693 and lasted about seven and a half hours.

Shakespeare's verse was drastically altered and reduced, his story being confined to the quarrel between Oberon and Titania, the fairies and the comedy of the rustics. Each of his scenes was followed by a splendid transformation and *divertissement* with ballets and singing.

Robert Helpmann as Oberon, costume design by Michael Ayrton, *The Fairy Queen,* The Royal Opera House, Covent Garden, 1946. (Victoria and Albert Museum)

The Fairy Queen had been largely forgotten, until Constant Lambert's lavish revival in 1946. The full Sadler's Wells Ballet under the direction of Frederick Ashton, and many members of the newly founded Covent Garden Opera Company took part. Michael Ayrton, who designed the costumes and scenery—including fairy forests, enchanted lakes with real fountains and a Chinese garden—was inspired by Inigo Jones and had a real feeling for 17th century sumptuousness and spectacle.

Benjamin Britten (1913–76): *A Midsummer Night's Dream*, Aldeburgh Jubilee Hall, 1960
Benjamin Britten, who had always loved *A Midsummer Night's Dream*, composed his opera of the same name for the Aldeburgh Jubilee Festival in 1960. The entire composition was completed in seven months. He and Peter Pears reduced the complex plot but kept faithfully to Shakespeare's words.

The fairies, especially Oberon, are of prime importance, and are the framework of the opera. They are 'very different from the innocent nothings that often appear in productions of Shakespeare,' said Britten in *The Observer*. He indicated the mystery of the forest in his music, and used a different orchestral texture for each of the groups of protagonists: lovers, rustics and fairies. The latter are accompanied by harp and percussion and as they are Titania's guards they sometimes have martial music. Puck, whom Britten represented as 'amoral but quite innocent . . . doesn't sing but only speaks and tumbles about.' The mischief of Puck and Oberon is indicated by the brass.

The scenery and costumes, designed by John Piper who worked closely with Britten, were in total harmony with the music. Piper had been struck by the greenness of most settings for the play, in spite of the fact that it takes place at night. He had been studying oriental wash drawings while hearing the early stages of Britten's composition. Recently, Piper wrote that both of these influences and summer nights suggested to him 'shades of diluted Chinese ink, with sometimes additions of Chinese white, making tones of silver grey. I still find that these, for me, marry reasonably well with this particular music.' Britten himself had, in fact, been researching into eastern music, and its influence is heard in his *A Midsummer Night's Dream*.

On stage, Piper's designs enhanced the air of mystery and dream. There were gauzes and giant plants dwarfing the protagonists, and fairies in variegated costumes in the colours of the forest.

The first new production of Britten's work was given at Covent Garden in 1961. For this, Piper made new designs.

A scene from Benjamin Britten's *A Midsummer Night's Dream,* designed by John Piper, The Royal Opera House, Covent Garden, 1961. (Royal Opera House Archives, Covent Garden)

Below
Anthony Dowell as Oberon in Sir Frederick Ashton's *The Dream,* The Royal Opera House, Covent Garden, 1979. (Royal Opera House Archives, Covent Garden)

Frederick Ashton (b. 1904): *The Dream*, Royal Opera House, Covent Garden, 1964

Frederick Ashton's one-act ballet *The Dream* was created for the celebrations of Shakespeare's four hundredth anniversary. Ashton used the central plot of *A Midsummer Night's Dream*: the fairies in the wood, the lovers and the rustics. Danced to an arrangement of Mendelssohn's music, the magical ballet captures the whole spirit of Shakespeare's play both in the characterisation and incidents. The roles of Oberon and Titania were created for Anthony Dowell and Antoinette Sibley.

NON-SHAKESPEARIAN FAIRIES

In the 19th century, a plethora of fairies appeared on the stage. Apart from the lavish Shakespearian productions, they were to be seen in extravaganzas, fairy operas, pantomimes and ballets, many of which were elaborate scenic spectacles.

Fairy Opera

Weber composed the fairy opera *Oberon: or the Elf-King's Oath* for Covent Garden. It was first performed in April 1821. The story was taken from Weiland's 'wild and gorgeous' poem *Oberon*. It had been dramatized by J. R. Planché, who excelled in the extravaganza and burlesque. Inevitably, the libretto was not perfectly suited to Weber's music, which was the surpassing glory of the evening, or to the performers who were primarily singers, not actors.

In Planché's libretto, Oberon, King of Fairyland, quarrels with his queen on the subject of female constancy, which he claims does not exist. He refuses to make his peace with her until a 'constant couple' is discovered. Sir Huon is a knight banished from France by Charlemagne until he brings back Rieza, daughter of the Caliph of Baghdad. On Sir Huon's journey, Oberon appears to him and, by Oberon's magic, Sir Huon and Rieza meet in a dream and fall in love. Oberon furnishes Sir Huon with a magic bowl and ivory horn, which enable him to overcome all his difficulties and finally return to France, triumphant, with his bride.

Of the first performance of *Oberon*, the critic from *The News* wrote, 'It had hardly commenced, when the magic power of the Composer was manifest; there was soon the agreeable stillness, and charming breathing of fabled fairyland.' *The News* claimed that nearly £6,000 had been spent on the elaborate scenery and costumes, and that the opera had been so eagerly anticipated that the crowds 'produced an overflow in all parts of the theatre'.

Of all 19th-century fairy operas, the most enduring favourite is *Iolanthe, or the Peer and Peri*, by W. S. Gilbert and Sir Arthur Sullivan. It was first produced at the Savoy Theatre in 1882. In this comic satire against the legislature, the author presented the inhabitants of Fairyland versus the Lord Chancellor and his Peers.

Iolanthe has been banished from Fairyland for marrying a mortal, the Lord Chancellor, and lives at the bottom of a stream. Her half-human son Strephon, a fairy down to the waist, is in love with a Ward in Chancery. A whimsical plot unfolds and its attendant difficulties are finally resolved when all the fairies marry Peers and the Fairy Queen marries the Sentry.

NEVER ACTED.

Theatre Royal, Covent-Garden,

This present WEDNESDAY, *April* 12, 1826.

Will be performed *(for the first time)* a Grand Romantic and Fairy OPERA, in three acts, (Founded on WIELAND's celebrated Poem) entitled

OBERON:
OR,
THE ELF-KING's OATH.

With entirely new Music, Scenery, Machinery, Dresses and Decorations.

The OVERTURE and the whole of the MUSIC composed by

CARL MARIA VON WEBER,

Who will preside this Evening in the Orchestra.

The CHORUS (under the direction of Mr. WATSON,) has been greatly augmented.
The DANCES composed by Mr. AUSTIN.
The Scenes painted by Mess. GRIEVE, PUGH, T. and W. GRIEVE, LUPPINO, and assistants.
The Machinery by Mr. E. SAUL. The Aerial Machinery, Transformations & Decorations by Mess. BRADWELL.
The Dresses by Mr PALMER, Miss EGAN, and assistants.

Fairies.

Oberon, *King of the Fairies,* Mr. C. BLAND,   Puck, Miss H. CAWSE,
Titania, *Queen of the Fairies,* Miss SMITH.

Franks.

Charlemagne, *King of the Franks,* Mr. AUSTIN,
Sir Huon, *of Bourdeaux, Duke of Guienne,*............Mr. BRAHAM,
Sherasmin, *his Squire,*...............Mr. FAWCETT.

Arabians.

Haroun-Al-Rashchid, *Caliph of Bagdad,* Mr. CHAPMAN,
Baba-Khan, *a Saracenic Prince,* Mr. BAKER,   Hassan, *Master of a Vessel,* Mr. J. ISAACS,
Hamet, Mr. EVANS,   Amrou, M. ATKINS,
Reiza, *Daughter of the Caliph,*...........Miss PATON,
Fatima, Madame VESTRIS,
Namouna, *Fatima's Grandmother,* Mrs. DAVENPORT.

Tunisians.

Almansor, *Emir of Tunis,*......Mr. COOPER,
Abdallah, *a Corsair,* Mr. HORREBOW,   Slave, Mr. TINNEY,
Roshana, *Wife of Almansor,*..........Miss LACY,
Nadina, *a female Slave,* Mrs. WILSON.
Officers, Soldiers, Slaves, &c. of the different Courts,———Fairies, Sprites, &c.

Order of the Scenery :

OBERON'S BOWER,

With the VISION.   Painted by Mr. Grieve.

Distant View of Bagdad, and the adjacent Country on the Banks of the Tigris,
By Sunset.   Grieve

INTERIOR of NAMOUNA's COTTAGE,   T. Grieve
VESTIBULE and TERRACE in the HAREM of the CALIPH, overlooking the Tigris.   W. Grieve
GRAND BANQUETTING CHAMBER of HAROUN.   T. Grieve
GARDENS of the PALACE.   Pugh

PORT OF ASCALON.

RAVINE amongst the ROCKS of a DESOLATE ISLAND.
The Haunt of the Spirits of the Storm.   Designed by Bradwell, and painted by Pugh.

Perforated Cavern on the Beach,

With the OCEAN—in a STORM—a CALM—by SUNSET—
Twilight—Starlight—and Moonlight.   T. Grieve

Exterior of Gardener's House in the Pleasure Grounds of the Emir of Tunis.   Grieve
Hall and Gallery in Almansor's Palace.   W. Grieve
MYRTLE GROVE in the GARDENS of the EMIR.   Pugh
GOLDEN SALOON in the KIOSK of ROSHANA.   W. Grieve.
The Palace and Gardens, by Moonlight.   Grieve.
COURT of the HAREM.   Pugh.
HALL of ARMS in the Palace of Charlemagne.   Grieve & Luppino.

The Opera is published, & may be had in the Theatre, & of Mess. Hunt & Clarke, 38, Tavistock-street, Covent-garden

To which will be added (23d time) a NEW PIECE, in one act, called

THE SCAPE-GOAT.

Old Eustace,   Mr. BLANCHARD,   Charles,   Mr. COOPER,
Ignatius Polyglot,   Mr. W. FARREN,   Robin,   Mr. MEADOWS,
Molly Maggs,   Miss JONES,   Harriet,   Miss A. JONES.

W. REYNOLDS, Printer, 9. Denmark-Court, Strand.

Playbill for the first production of *Oberon: or the Elf King's Oath*, at Covent Garden, music by Carl Maria von Weber, 12th April 1826. (Royal Opera House Archives, Covent Garden)

The production showed some amusing surprises. At a given cue, the fairies (who wore tiny batteries on their backs concealed by their long hair), switched on electric lights on their foreheads: an imaginative use of this newly invented form of lighting. In the finale, all the mortals turned into fairies and all sprouted wings—the Sentry, the Peers and the Lord Chancellor himself.

1. Leila (Miss Julia Gwynne), One of Strephon's Aunts.—2. Private Willis, Grenadier Guard (Mr. Manners).—3. Iolanthe (Miss Jessie Bond) : The Life and Soul of Fairyland, Returning from Penal Servitude.—4. A Very Influential Fairy (Miss Alice Barnett).—5. Strephon, M.P. (Mr. R. Temple).—6. Act II. Fairy Invasion of Palace Yard.—7. Phyllis, a Ward of Court (Miss Braham), Sees Nothing in the Coronets of Lords Mountararat and Tolluller (Messrs. Barrington and Lely).—8. A Highly Susceptible Chancellor (Mr. George Grossmith).—9. "Faint Heart Never Won Fair Lady."—10. Pillars of the British Nation.

Scenes from the first production
of Gilbert and Sullivan's
Iolanthe, The Savoy Theatre,

1882. Picture from *The Graphic*.
(Theatre Museum, Victoria and
Albert Museum)

Pantomime

The good fairy has always played a significant role in pantomime: in the early 19th century, by converting the protagonists into the characters of the harlequinade; in later years, by her influence in the fairy tale plot, which had become the major part of the performance. There were often good and bad fairies in the same pantomime, and even multitudes of fairies.

The second half of the 19th century saw the golden age of pantomime, but it was an extremely popular holiday entertainment for all classes throughout the century. The pantomime inherited by the early 19th century was a two-part entertainment. The subject of the first, much shorter half was taken from a source such as a myth, fairy tale or nursery rhyme. The second part was a harlequinade originating from the *Commedia dell'Arte*. The basic plot of the first half was that of an authoritarian father preventing his beautiful daughter from marrying her lover, and presenting her with an unsuitable suitor in his stead. At this stage, the good fairy entered. To protect the lovers, the fairy transformed them into Harlequin and Columbine, and the other characters into Pantaloon, Clown and Lover, who pursued them in a knockabout low comedy full of antics. Finally, the good fairy intervened to reconcile the lovers with their pursuers and the pantomime had a spectacular ending in the splendid dwelling place of the good fairy, where everyone praised happiness and love.

By the 1830s, audiences had become more interested in the introductory shows and the harlequinade began to decline, until the former became a self-contained play and the harlequinade an irrelevant extra. The good fairies now demonstrated their benevolent influence on behalf of the hero and heroine within what had been the introductory section, without using the harlequinade scene.

From the 1840s, the pantomime was performed solely at Christmas, as an entertainment for the whole family, but especially for children. Its content was altered accordingly. Scenery and transformation effects became more spectacular, costumes were created by important designers, and the plot became simpler, with something of a moral emphasis. For instance, evil spirits were seen in gloomy environs which contrasted strikingly with the dazzling settings which surrounded the good fairy.

After 1850, famous fairy stories, sometimes two or three used in combination and with plenty of additional comic material, became an increasingly popular source for pantomime subject matter. An important role of the fairies was now to bring about spectacular scenic transformations. A memorable example was *The Sleeping Beauty and the Beast*, written by J. Hickory Wood and Arthur Collins, and shown at Drury Lane in 1900. While Beauty slept, the Fairy Queen entered the palace of sleep. After her words:

> To Beauty, in her dream I wish to show,
> How year by year the swift days come and go,

a series of dazzling transformations took the audience through the seasons—Spring, Summer, Autumn and Winter.

Charles Wilhelm: costume design for one of the twelve Fairy Godmothers in *Sleeping Beauty,* 1886. (University of Bristol, Theatre Collection)

Grand Transformation Scene
from *The Island of Jewels,* 1849.
(Victoria and Albert Museum)

Usually, the finale of Part One was the grandest transformation. It was often effected by the good fairy, revealing a magical land and was the excuse for a fairy ballet. A spectacular transformation was the ending of the fairy extravaganza *The Island of Jewels*, written by J. R. Planché in 1849, for which, as Planché recalled, William Beverley designed 'a novel yet exceedingly simple falling of the leaves of a palm tree, discovering six fairies supporting a coronet of jewels.'

Fairies in Ballet

The great age of Romantic ballet in England was from about 1830 until 1850. Ballet was at its most popular and enthralled a wide section of society, from Queen Victoria downwards. During these years, a number of European ballerinas of outstanding talent—notably Marie Taglioni, Carlotta Grisi and Fanny Cerrito—visited London. They created a sensation, eclipsing the male dancers, and the

101

image of the ballerina that they established lives on today.

Marie Taglioni gave her first London performance of *La Sylphide*, a ballet created for her by her choreographer father, in July 1832. It was an overwhelming success and she performed it on most of her visits to London. Taglioni, the supreme exemplar of the Romantic ballet, became inseparably linked with the title role in this work.

The Spirit, La Sylphide, and a Scotsman fall in love. He leaves his betrothed and they go into the forest, where she dies when he unwittingly places on her shoulders a scarf over which a sorceress has cast a fatal spell. Of Taglioni's London performance in 1837, the critic from *The Morning Post* wrote, 'She danced like a fairy . . . and dies as a Sylph should die, her tiny wings dropping from their place, her gentle form bending like a reed . . . fainting into death.'

Jules Perrot, the greatest choreographer of the time,

Marie Taglioni as La Sylphide, lithograph by J.H. Lynch from a drawing by A.E. Chalon, 1845. (Theatre Museum, Victoria and Albert Museum)

Lucile Grahn in *Eoline ou la Dryade,* lithograph by Edward Morton after S.M. Joy, 1845. (Mary Evans Picture Library)

worked in London in the 1840s. He was instrumental in raising the English ballet to a short reign of pre-eminence. He choreographed ballets for the greatest dancers of the day, who added to masterly technique a creative characterisation of the roles they danced.

During this period, very significant innovations in the ballerina's technique were made, the most revolutionary of which was the development of the 'pointe'. Now she could dance on the very tips of her toes, scarcely touching the ground. This technique enhanced the roles she played, many of which were ideal creatures, ethereal and mysterious, including a variety of fairies: naiads, dryads, ondines, nymphs and sylphs. These were beings, inspired by Romantic imagination and literature, which floated gracefully across the stage.

Perrot's first major choreographic work was *Ondine*, danced by Fanny Cerrito in 1843. It was a stupendous success. Full of atmosphere, it included naiads appearing beneath the lake. The glory of the evening was an enchanting *pas de l'ombre* in which Ondine, the water sprite, danced by moonlight with her shadow.

In 1845, Perrot created *Eoline, ou La Dryade*. Lucile Grahn danced Eoline, the half-dryad, half-human who falls in love with a mortal and dies on her wedding day, when a jealous gnome sets alight the tree which sustains her life.

These ballets were produced on the most grandiose scale, with magnificent sets and ingenious theatrical devices made by the ablest stage designers. But their overwhelming popularity did not last, as the combination of talents which sustained these ballets faded and financial backing was no longer forthcoming. Opera was becoming fashionable and in such entertainments, ballet was relegated to the position of a supplementary *divertissement*.

Margot Fonteyn as Cinderella, Annette Page as the Fairy Godmother, David Blair as the Prince in *Cinderella*, Covent Garden, 1965.

Carlotta Brianza as Carabosse in *The Sleeping Princess,* The Alhambra, 1921. (Victoria and Albert Museum)

'I always return to Petipa over everything . . . people sometimes find me at a matinée of *The Sleeping Beauty*, which I have seen literally hundreds of times. And they ask me what I'm doing and I say "having a private lesson",' said Sir Frederick Ashton, in an interview with John Selwyn Gilbert. Indeed, in the structure of his own famous ballet *Cinderella*, based on another Perrault fairy tale, the influence of Petipa and Ivanov is apparent.

Ballet has enjoyed a revival in England, especially since the last war, and fairy tales have been a rich source of inspiration. Many perennial favourites, regularly performed by English companies, were originally products of Russian genius. Fairies from Russian ballets have transcended national boundaries. The Sugar Plum Fairy in the Kingdom of Sweets from *The Nutcracker*, choreographed by Ivanov in 1892 to music by Tchaikovsky, is a particular favourite.

The famous gallery of fairies in *The Sleeping Beauty* is familiar to many audiences: the Fairies of the Crystal Fountain, of the Enchanted Garden, of the Woodland Glade, of the Songbirds, of the Golden Vine, of the Lilac, and the wicked Fairy Carabosse. The version of *The Sleeping Beauty* that we know was choreographed by Petipa in 1890 to music by Tchaikovsky. It was first staged in London under the title *The Sleeping Princess* in a magnificent but financially disastrous production at the Alhambra Theatre by Diaghilev's *Ballets Russes*, with costumes and scenery designed by Léon Bakst. *The Times* reported on the Royal visit to this ballet in December 1921, 'The King and Queen, and as many of their loyal subjects as could conveniently be squeezed into the Alhambra, spent a couple of hours in that region of fairyland which the Russian ballet has made particularly its own. Their Majesties . . . arrived at Fairyland (by the Charing Cross Road entrance . . .).'

It was also with *The Sleeping Beauty*, this time at Covent Garden in 1946, that London saw the first appearance of a British ballet company on a large scale. Margot Fonteyn was superb as Princess Aurora and Robert Helpmann was Prince Florimund. The settings were by Oliver Messel.

A ballet in the true romantic mood that still retains its popularity is *Les Sylphides*. Choreographed by Fokine, to music by Chopin, it was first performed by Diaghilev's Company in Paris in 1909. The title was inspired by *La Sylphide*. This one act ballet is pure dance without a story. The ballerinas, dressed *à la Taglioni* in full white skirts, are sylphs who dance in a moonlit glade accompanied by one male figure.

Margot Fonteyn and Robert Helpmann in *Sleeping Beauty*, Act II, Covent Garden, 1946. (Royal Opera House Archives, Covent Garden)

We have not totally abandoned fairies, even in our logical and scientific age. Distilled and transmuted into the artificial medium of the theatre, fairies still captivate us with their magic. Young children of today still believe in pantomime fairies: Tinkerbell, who usually appears as a flickering light, delights hundreds of young visitors to *Peter Pan* each year. Favourite fairy stories are performed as ballets, and creations of genius and originality continue to be inspired by the most famous fairies of the stage, which were created by Shakespeare almost four centuries ago.

Fairy Painting and Illustration

Fairy painting and illustration was a late development in the history of man's relations with the 'Good People'. In deference to their powers, stories were told and chronicles written of their exploits long before any attempt was made to describe their appearance graphically. Ingenious theories have been put forward to support the appearance of sprites and goblins either as subject matter or as marginal illuminations in early manuscripts, but these cannot be proved. Usually, the tiny winged beings found in manuscripts such as the Utrecht Psalter represent abstract concepts rather than fairies; they derive from classical prototypes and representations of the human soul. The little creatures that appear in marginalia, however, are

Previous page
Villanis: *Farfalla.* The title derives from a corruption of 'firefly'. (Editions Graphiques, London)

Fairies Dancing, an illustration from an old English chapbook. (Fortean Picture Library)

products of the same fertile imaginations that designed the gargoyle demons that ornament our Romanesque and Gothic churches; they are the direct descendants of the monsters found in Celtic bestiaries and such manuscripts as the Book of Kells.

Among the first known visual representations of fairies are those which appeared in 1555, in a book published in Rome, *De Gentibus Septentrionalibus* (A History of the Scandinavian Peoples) by Olaus Magnus, Archbishop of Uppsala. It contains a remarkable series of woodcut illustrations, including several of supernatural subjects. One of these shows a knight dismounted from his horse, being enticed by fairies to join them inside a hollow hill. The fairies are of less than adult size and wear contemporary costume. Notwithstanding their Scandinavian origins, these illustrations bear a remarkable similarity to observations made in the writings of Robert Kirk, the 17th century Minister of Aberfoyle.

The first artistic impressions of British fairies are found in woodcut illustrations to chapbooks and tracts of the early 17th century and take the form of dancing circles of miniature black stick-figures. Such a fairy ring can be seen moving around the eponymous hobgoblin on the title page for *Robin Goodfellow, His Mad Prankes and Merry Jests* of 1639. They are differentiated as men and women although they all wear high hats. Robin himself is shown in the guise of a lustful satyr with a goat's horns, legs and hooves. A similar fairy ring is shown in the frontispiece to Bovet's *Pandaemonium or the Devil's Cloister* of 1684, where it is depicted alongside other manifestations of the devil. Among more accomplished representations dating from the same period are the designs by Inigo Jones for the costumes worn by the fays in Jonson's masque, *Oberon the Fairy Prince* of 1611. In Jones's conception, the fairies have a rather grotesque goblin-like appearance, while Oberon himself is portrayed as a classical prince.

Very little interest was shown in representing fairies during the early and middle 18th century. Apart from the occasional book illustration, there is only one work of note: a most unusual painting of the mid-eighteenth century which shows a countryman, perhaps Milton's 'belated peasant' witnessing *Fairies dancing on the green by moonlight*. It was commissioned from either Hogarth or Hayman to decorate a supper-box at the Vauxhall gardens.

In the late 18th century, a positive mixture of patriotism and self-interest prompted John Boydell, the owner of a successful print gallery, to commission work from leading contemporary artists to illustrate the writings of 'England's greatest national writer', William Shakespeare. Among the contributions was *Puck*, painted by Sir Joshua Reynolds in

Henry Fuseli: *Titania and Bottom,* 1875. (The Tate Gallery)

1789, which shows a plump and impish child with slant eyes and pointed ears, perched on a toadstool and clutching a bunch of pansies, the 'love-in-idleness' of Oberon's lines. Henry Fuseli painted two scenes from the play between 1780 and 1790: *Titania and Bottom,* which is now at the Tate Gallery, and *Titania's Awakening,* which is in a collection in Switzerland. Fuseli interpreted the characters in terms of erotic fantasy dreams or nightmares, indulging in an almost surreal play of the imagination. In both paintings, the fairy folk assume a variety of sizes and roles. There are sophisticated temptresses in contemporary dress drawn from medieval romance, misshapen dwarves and tiny flying figures. It has been suggested that the lady on the right of *Titania and Bottom,* who holds a wizened, bearded figure on a string, is actually Nimuë leading the captive Merlin. This teeming variety of creation was to prove influential later in the 19th century with the work of such artists as Maclise and Paton.

The sprite lounging at the bottom left of *Titania and Bottom,* with its finger to its lips, could well be identified as Moth. Its winged headpiece is reminiscent of the wings that sprout from the head of one of the dancing fairies in

Daniel Maclise: *The Faun and the Fairies, c*1834. (Private collection)

112

W. Blake: *Oberon, Titania and Puck with Fairies dancing.* (The Tate Gallery)

G. Cruikshank: *The Elves and the Shoe maker,* illustration to *German Popular Stories,* 1823. (Raymond Watkinson)

William Blake's *Oberon, Titania and Puck with fairies dancing*, painted around 1785, which also belongs to the Tate Gallery. Here, Oberon and Titania appear to be of ancient British origin, while Puck is Bacchanalian in his dress and the fairies are clad in clinging draperies of classical type.

Around 1820, Blake also illustrated the fairy passage from *L'Allegro* in a watercolour which is now in the Pierpont Morgan Library. It depicts the Fairy Mab eating the junkets, the woman who was 'pincht and pull'd', and the horned hobgoblin rejecting the drudgery to which he is subjected.

During the 1790's, George Romney executed several scenes from *A Midsummer Night's Dream*, for one of which Emma, Lady Hamilton posed as a coquettish and very corporeal Titania. In the background of *Titania, Puck and the Changeling*, in the National Gallery of Ireland, are suspended small, chubby fairies, who resemble to some extent the sylphs created by Thomas Stothard between 1798 and 1804 to illustrate Pope's *The Rape of the Lock*. Here we find

Daniel Maclise: illustration to Dickens's *The Chimes, c*1845. (Victoria and Albert Museum)

116

Sir Joseph Noel Paton: *The Reconciliation of Oberon and Titania,* 1847. (National Gallery of Scotland, Edinburgh)

the *putto*-like sylphs sporting a variety of wings, from large, butterfly appendages to stubby little fins sprouting from their shoulders. Although fairies gradually lost their resemblance to Neo-Classical cherubs, a precedent had now been set for the appearance of their wings.

Fairies appear with and without wings in the delicate drawings of W. H. Brooke. He contributed illustrations to Crofton Croker's *Fairy Legends and Traditions of the South of Ireland* and Keightley's *The Fairy Mythology,* both published in 1828, and was also active as a caricaturist. He was succeeded in both capacities by George Cruickshank. Cruickshank, who began his career as a political cartoonist, was responsible for the etched illustrations for the first English edition of the Grimms' *German Popular Stories,* published in 1823. He also contributed illustrations to Crofton Croker and to Keightley and from 1853 to 1864 proceeded to publish his own *Fairy Library.* As a child, Cruickshank had learned how to etch plates, and he was capable of producing extraordinarily minute details in his depictions.

117

George Cruikshank: etching
from Thomas Keightley's *Fairy
Mythology,* 1828. (Alister
Mathews, Bournemouth)

He executed several individual prints in which the fairies
become instruments of satire—for instance, *The Fairy Connoisseurs,* in which they are shown inspecting giant paintings. He could achieve remarkable vitality in his
watercolours; for example, he skilfully suggests the speed
at which the fairies dance in his ant's eye view of fairy
revels, *A Fantasy* (Victoria & Albert Museum).

The 1840's marked the beginning of the Golden Age of
fairy painting. A few individual works of note were produced before this, among them the watercolour scenes from
A Midsummer Night's Dream (at Yale's Mellon Center and
at Oldham Museum and Art Gallery) by Francis Danby.
The Oldham painting of about 1832 portrays the meeting
and quarrel of Oberon and Titania, which takes place in
a clearing among tree roots. It is painted with great delicacy in a limited range of muted colours, conveying the
haunting atmosphere of a glade illuminated only by moon-
shine and glow-worms.

Richard Doyle: illustration to
Mark Lemon's *The Enchanted
Doll,* 1849. (Ronald Horton)

E. Griset: illustration to Lord
Brabourne's *The Little Gentleman.* (Raymond Watkinson)

Jeremy Maas has noted in his germinal essay on fairy
painting, published in *Victorian Painters* (1969), that the
hard-headed materialism of the Victorian era was
accompanied by a remarkable degree of interest in the
intangible spirit world. Clerics and academics were among
the founder members of the Society for Psychical Research
and a belief in the supernatural was taken very seriously.
At the same time, there was a new wave of interest in
Celtic folklore and the denizens of Fairyland, an interest
that was shared by the monarch herself, who bought a
number of fairy paintings.

Two of the greatest fairy painters, Daniel Maclise and

Richard Doyle: *A Fairy Ring.*
(Private collection, Maas
Gallery photograph)

Sir Joseph Noel Paton, were appropriately of Celtic origin. Maclise was an Irish artist who began his work in England, like many, by contributing illustrations to Crofton Croker's *Fairy Legends* (the 1826 edition). He also provided illustrations to the 1845 edition of Thomas Moore's *Irish Melodies*, and for *The Chimes* (1844) and *The Cricket on the Hearth* (1845) by Charles Dickens. All of these drawings teem with the activities of the fairy folk. Notable among Maclise's fairy paintings are the oval *The Faun and the Fairies*, an early work of about 1834, in which fairy couples entwine and dance to music played on the pan pipes by a sardonic faun in their midst; and *Undine*, which was exhibited at the Royal Academy in 1844 and was bought by Queen Victoria as a present for Prince Albert. In this painting a cascade of fairy bodies again provides a framework for the main action of the popular German story, in which a young knight, Huldbrand, escorts his nymph-wife through the wild forests.

Sir Joseph Noel Paton spent almost all his life in his native Dunfermline, exhibiting his work at the Royal Scottish Academy. He painted two epic scenes (both in the National Gallery of Scotland) which were based on *A Midsummer Night's Dream*, but largely improvised from his own imagination: *The Reconciliation of Oberon and Titania*, shown in 1847, and *The Quarrel of Oberon and Titania*, which was begun earlier but not exhibited until 1850. The latter was hailed as 'The Picture of the Exhibition', and Lewis Carroll reported enthusiastically that he had counted 165 fairies in it. There is indeed in both paintings an abundance of fairy life, of all shapes and descriptions. There are water nymphs, flower fairies, goblins and sprites; fairies dancing, flying, making love or taunting each other or small animals. Yet the overall prettiness of both paintings is tempered by the touches of cruelty that still abound; the owl that flies captive in *The Quarrel*, for example, is about to be killed in the foreground of *The Reconciliation*. Fairyland has not yet been completely tamed. Paton's third fairy masterpiece, *A Fairy Raid* (Glasgow City Art Gallery) was not completed until 1867. A tour-de-force, it is painted with far more subtlety and imbued with greater magic than either of its predecessors. It shows a successful hunting party of fairies, returning to their home among the standing stones with their captives, human children. It is interesting to note that Paton achieved equal fame as a religious painter.

John Simmons: *Scene from A Midsummer Night's Dream, Act III scene I,* 'The honey-bags steal from the humble bees'. (Private collection, Maas Gallery photograph)

Robert Huskisson: *The Mother's Blessing.* (Private collection, Maas Gallery photograph)

123

124

William Shackleton: *The Nymph of Malham Cove, 'Moonlight Idyll'.* (Towneley Hall Art Gallery and Museums, Burnley)

Certain artists shamelessly took advantage of the vogue for fairy painting to depict the female nude. Paton himself took obvious delight in the classically proportional figures of Oberon and Titania in his scenes from *A Midsummer Night's Dream*, while later artists such as John Simmons used Shakespearian themes as a thinly veiled excuse for producing provocative images of shapely Victorian beauties. The mysterious artist Heatherley took the erotic implications of the genre to an extreme by causing his extremely buxom nude fairies to disport themselves on giant mushrooms.

After the success of *The Reconciliation*, Paton's friend, the photographer Octavius Hill, warned him 'The asinine multitude . . . might say this, because you painted fairies as they were never painted before, that argues that you can

Thomas Heatherley: *Fairy seated on a Mushroom.* (Private collection, Maas Gallery photograph)

Richard Dadd: *Songe de la Fantasie,* 1864. (Fitzwilliam Museum, Cambridge)

FAIRY FELLAS MASTER STROKE SO LYNSEY SAYS.

do nothing else and that you are raving mad.' It is sobering to reflect upon the link between the creation of these fantasy paintings and mental illness. Indeed, one of the most famous and obsessive of fairy painters, Richard Dadd, spent the greater part of his life in a series of asylums, suffering from schizophrenia. Another artist whose notebooks are peppered with fairies and who suffered from alcoholism and epilepsy was Charles Doyle, while the vivid

126

and perplexing scenes of dreams and fairies that sprang from the imagination of John Anster Fitzgerald caused his sanity to be held in doubt.

By 1841, Richard Dadd had already illustrated books of ballads and exhibited paintings on fairy themes. Confined after murdering his father in 1843, he was to enlarge upon them in his sadly unnatural maturity. His best known work is probably *The Fairy Feller's Master Stroke* (in the Tate Gallery), which occupied the artist during the years 1855–64, spent at Bethlem Hospital. The painting describes a very complex slice of Fairyland. A watercolour replica, *Songe de la Fantasie* (from the Fitzwilliam Museum, Cambridge), was executed after his arrival at Broadmoor in 1864. He made a great number of fairy works of varying quality throughout his life, but it was his early work that proved most influential to younger artists such as Robert Huskisson, whose *Midsummer Night's Fairies* and *Come Unto These Yellow Sands* are closely modelled on prototypes by Dadd.

Like Dadd's work, Fitzgerald's paintings are executed with an exacting attention to detail and fall into two types. There are those that deal with the strange world of the human dreamer and those that show Fairyland, where the inhabitants are shown boasting, attacking a robin in its nest, or feasting. *The Fairy Banquet* and *Fairies in a Bird's Nest* are exquisite examples of his art. They have an

Richard Doyle: *Sprites on a Cliff.* (Private collection)

John Anster Fitzgerald: *Fairies in a Bird's Nest.* (Private collection, Maas Gallery photograph)

extraordinary intensity of colour. These minute examinations of the daily life of fairy folk were extremely popular with the practical, materialistic yet credulous Victorians who yearned for spiritual experience. Fitzgerald also executed a series of large fairy subjects for Christmas editions of the *Illustrated London News*.

The Doyle family were most prolific in their output of fairy painting and illustration. John Doyle, the caricaturist,

Richard Doyle: illustration to *Dick Doyle's Journal*, 1885. (Ronald Horton)

Arthur Hughes: illustrations to Christina Rossetti's *Sing Song, A Nursery Rhyme Book,* 1872. (Raymond Watkinson)

had seven children, all of whom inherited his artistic gifts. Richard followed his father into the offices of *Punch* until his growing Catholic conscience forbade him. He produced the first illustrations to Ruskin's *The King of the Golden River* in 1851, but his greatest works are the wood engravings he made in 1870 for *In Fairyland*, which accompanied a poem by William Allingham. His work exhibits much of the intricacy of Paton's, but purged of any sinister implications. Richard's younger brother, Charles, was never a professional painter, but he portrayed charming, if homely, fairy girls in relation to incongruous objects or animals, displaying his quirky humour.

During the middle years of the century, a small number

129

Arthur Hughes: illustration to Christina Rossetti's *Sing Song, A Nursery Rhyme Book*

of works that pertained to fairies were executed by members of the Pre-Raphaelite Brotherhood. In 1849, Millais painted *Ferdinand lured by Ariel* (in the Makins Collection), a rare excursion by him into Fairyland. Ariel exhibits the form of a human child, although poison-green in hue, while his fairy companions share his complexion but are more grotesque in appearance. Arthur Hughes painted an interesting rejoinder. In his *Ferdinand and Ariel* (in the Munro Collection), the prince is shown listening to empty air: the spirit has been left invisible. Hughes was also responsible for some inspired illustrations to Allingham's *The Music Masters* in 1855 and to Christina Rossetti's *Sing Song* of

Dante Gabriel Rossetti: detail from title page to Christina Rossetti's *Goblin Market and Other Poems*, 1865.

Dante Gabriel Rossetti: 'The Maids of Elfen Mere', illustration to William Allingham's *The Music Masters, a love story and two series of Day and Night Songs*, 1855

1872, in which one of his drawings, of fairies dancing in the moonlight, shows an interesting similarity to the silhouetted figures of the old chapbooks. Dante Gabriel Rossetti is notable for his wood engravings for Allingham's *The Maids of Elfinmere* and for his sister's poem *Goblin Market*, which was later illustrated even more disturbingly by Laurence Housman.

There were many other contemporary illustrators of note. A prolific artist whose work deserves to be better known was Eleanor Vere Boyle, or E.V.B. She painted and drew few fairies in the accepted sense, but used her own children as models for the diminutive creatures who inhabit the countryside of *Woodland Gossip* (1864), Carové's *The Story Without an End* (1868) and Andersen's *Fairy Stories*. Of the next generation, Burne Jones's earliest illustration, found on the title page of *The Fairy Family* by Archibald Maclaren, owes much to the work of Dicky Doyle. Walter Crane executed work on the theme of fairies in a variety of media. He produced tile designs such as *Flora's Train*—which were made by Pilkington's Company in 1902, designs for wallpapers such as *The Fairy Garden* of 1890, and numerous book illustrations, including those for the delightful *The First of May: A Fairy Masque*. He was much taken with the theme of the personification of flowers and celebrated it in the delightful drawings for *Flora's Feast* (1889), *Queen Summer or the Tournament of the Rose* (1891) and *A Floral Fantasy in an Old English Garden* (1899).

John Batten and Henry Justice Ford were fellow students at the Slade School who both became successful illustrators. Batten is chiefly remembered for his contributions to Joseph Jacobs' *English Fairy Tales* and *Celtic Fairy Tales*, published in the 1890s. Ford is known for his work executed for many of Andrew Lang's coloured *Fairy Books* of the

Eleanor Vere Boyle: *When the Spring Begins* from *The Story without an End* from the German of Carové, 1868

Overleaf
Richard Doyle: *Triumphal march of the Elf-King* from *In Fairyland* by William Allingham, 1870

The Hobgoblin laughed till his sides ached

H.J. Ford: 'The Hobgoblin laughed till his sides ached', illustration to *The Snow-Queen*, from *The Pink Fairy Book* edited by Andrew Lang, 1901

LEIGHTON, BROS.

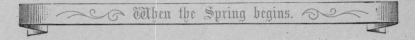
When the Spring begins.

same period. His drawings were to prove a major source of inspiration to Daisy Makeig Jones, the decorator of Wedgwood Fairyland Lustreware.

The final flowering of romantic book illustration was marked by the works of Charles and W. Heath Robinson, and of Arthur Rackham and Edmund Dulac. Charles Robinson was never able to study art full time, but he nevertheless achieved great success as the illustrator of such books as *The Water Babies*, fairy-tale collections and Oscar Wilde's *The Happy Prince* of 1913. He also executed a number of fairy paintings for which no source is apparent. W. Heath Robinson, who is principally remembered for his comical graphic inventions, was also the creator of wonderful illustrations for classic editions of *Danish Fairy Tales and Legends* by Hans Andersen, published in 1897,

Charles Robinson: *Fairy in an Autumn Glade*. (Drusilla and Colin White)

137

Frederick Cayley Robinson:
'The Dance of the Hours',
illustration to the Methuen
Edition of Maeterlinck's *The
Bluebird*, 1911. (Fitzwilliam
Museum, Cambridge)

Arthur Rackham: 'Midsummer
Fairies', illustration to *Lamb's
Tales from Shakespeare*, 1899.
(James Chesterman Collection)

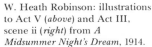

W. Heath Robinson: illustrations to Act V (*above*) and Act III, scene ii (*right*) from *A Midsummer Night's Dream*, 1914.

and a 1914 edition of *A Midsummer Night's Dream*, in which gossamer fairies of the utmost delicacy frolic with a most endearing, insect-like Puck.

Both Rackham and Dulac illustrated editions of Andersen's *Fairy Stories*, and Rackham painted a notable series of illustrations to *A Midsummer Night's Dream* in 1908. There is a charm about the work of both which smacks of another age and is well suited to the theme of Fairyland itself. Dulac was apt to orientalise the few fairies that he actually depicted; Rackham placed many of his creations firmly in the eighteenth century, a more elegant era.

Stylised and highly decorative fairies were occasionally produced by members of the Glasgow School such as Charles Rennie Mackintosh and Jessie M. King. In the work of Margaret and Frances Macdonald, however, self-consciousness of line and form often deprives their fairy subjects of any real meaning. Rackham, Dulac and the Robinsons, Harry Clarke and Warwick Goble continued to produce stylish fairy illustrations into the middle years of the 20th century, but the mantle of fairy painting was largely assumed by a number of well-meaning but rather whimsical ladies. These included Mabel Lucie Attwell,

John Dicksen Batten: 'Connia and the Fairy Maid', illustration for Jacob's *Celtic Fairy Tales*, 1892. (Michael Heseltine)

who created the memorable 'Boo-boos', pixies in green jump-suits, Cecily Mary Barker who extemporised on the theme of flower fairies, producing some for every season of the year, Margaret Tarrant, who proved a favourite in the nursery and Ida Outhwaite whose fairies were conceived in the Art Deco idiom.

The next, somewhat uncomfortable stage in the evolution of graphic fairy imagery took place on the silver screen rather than in book illustration. The Hungarian born Willy Pogany was one of several artists who took up the challenge offered by Hollywood and became art director for Warner's First National Studios. The supernatural creatures that appear in Walt Disney's early films, such as *Snow White* and *Fantasia*, show considerable dexterity and imagination but Barrie's Tinkerbell, as she is depicted in the cartoon of *Peter Pan* is a sorry creation. Until recently, fairy painting has been at a low ebb, and it was not until the still unfinished studies of *Titania* and *Puck* by Peter Blake appeared in the 1960s that a bold, new, contemporary image was created and we felt a stab of the old magic.

Mabel Lucie Attwell: illustration from *The Boo Boos at the Seaside*, c1920. (Mabel Lucie Attwell Ltd)

Charles Rennie Mackintosh:
Fairies, 1898. (Glasgow School of
Art)

Index

Page numbers in italic refer to pictures or to references in picture captions.

Absalon, John *51*
Aglio, Agostino *30*
Allegro, L' 64, 116
Allingham, William 70, 129, 130, 131, *131*, *134*
Anatomy of Melancholy, The 57, 88
Ancestral Voices 41
Andersen, Hans 67, 131, 137, 139
Ansorge, Peter 91
Argyll, Duke of 41
Ariel 46
Ariel on the Bat's Back 71
Arthur, King 49-50
Ashton, Sir Frederick 93, 95, *95*, 105
Assemblage of Fairytale and Nursery Rhyme Characters 9
Attwell, Mabel Lucie 19, 139, 140, *140*
Aubrey, John 17, 28
Ayrton, Michael *92*, 93

Bakst, Leon 106
Barker, Cecily Mary 19, 139, 140
Barrie, J.M. 13, 70, 96, 139
Bataille of Agincourt, The 60
Batten, John 132, *140*
Battle between King Oberon and the Pygmees, A 64
Beauty and the Beast 62, 67, *84*
Bechstein, Ludwig *56*
Belated Peasant, The *31*
Belle Dame Sans Mercie, La 66
Bell, Robert Anning *33*
Benthall, Michael 89
Berners, Lord 50
Bertin, Théodore-Pierre *50*
Beverley, Willliam 101
Blake, Peter 139, 140
Blake, William 28, *114*, 115, 116
Bluebird, The *138*
Blyton, Enid 70
Boo Boos at the Seaside, The *140*
Book of Kells, The 111
Bosch, Hieronymus 91
Bovet 111
Boydell, John 111
Boyle, Eleanor Vere 131, *133*
Brabourne, Lord *120*
Bray, Mrs 67
Brianza, Carlotta *105*
Briggs, Dr Katharine 66
Britannia's Pastorals 60
Britten, Benjamin 93, *94*
Brook, Peter 90, *90*
Brooke, W.H. 117
Browne, William 60
Bull, John 76
Burne Jones, Sir Edward Coley 131
Burton, Robert 57-58, 60, 64
Burton, William 60
Butterfly's Ball and the Grasshopper's Feast, The 68

Carové *133*
Carroll, Lewis 121

Cavendish, Margaret, Duchess of Newcastle 63-64
Celtic Fairy Tales 132, *140*
Cerrito, Fanny 101, 104
Certain Elegant Poems 66
Chalon, A.E. *102*
Chamberlayne, General William John *65*
Chat in the Playroom and Life at a Farmhouse 69
Chaucer, Geoffrey 14, 31, 49
Child, F.J. 68
Chimes, The *116*, 121
Chinon of England 60
Chopin, Frédéric 106
Cinderella 63, 69, *104*, 105
Clarke, Harry 140
Coleridge, Samuel T. 66
Collins, Arthur 99
Come unto these Yellow Sands 127
Coming of the Fairies, The 37
Confessio Amantis 49
Connia and the Fairy Maid 140
Corbet, Bishop 66
Corbett, Mary *26*
Cottingley Fairies, The 33-40, *34*
Crane, Walter *12*, *20*, 132, 139
Cricket on the Hearth, The 121
Croker, Crofton 67, 117, 121
Cruikshank, George *63*, *114*, 117-119, *Cruikshank's Fairy Library* 63
Cupid and Psyche 17

Dadd, Richard *18*, 19, 126, *126*
Daemonologie 57
Danby, Francis 119
Dance of the Hours, The *138*
Dance of the Pixies, The *61*
Danish Fairy Tales and Legends 137
D'Aulnoy, Comtesse 67
Dean, Basil 85
De Gentibus Septentrionalibus 111
de Morgan, Mary 69
de Murat, Mme 67
De Nugis Curialium 26
De Nymphis 14, 57
Description of the King and Queene of Fayries, A 58
de Villeneuve, Mme 67
Devine, George 88
Diaghilev, S. 106
Dick Doyle's Journal 128
Dickens, Charles 69, *116*, 121
Discoverie of Witchcraft, The 54, 56
Donne, John 60
Dowell, Anthony 95, *95*
Doyle, Sir Arthur Conan 33, 37, *38*
Doyle, Charles 126, 129
Doyle, John 128
Doyle, Richard *21*, *43*, *53*, *61*, 70, *119*, *121*, *127*, *128*, 129, 132, *134*
Drayton, Michael 60, 64
Dream, The 95, *95*
Dryad 27
Dulac, Edmund *9*, *84*, 137, 139, 140
Dymchurch Flit, The *45*

Elf Attendant on Bottom *48*
Elidor and the Golden Ball 24
Eloine, ou la Dryade *103*, 104
Elves and the Shoemaker, The *114*
Emma, Lady Hamilton 116
Emmerson, Henry Hetherington *40*
Enchanted Doll, The *119*
Endimion 51, 56
English and Scottish Popular Ballads 68

English Fairy Tales 132
'E.R.W.' 76
Evdokimova, Eva *107*
Evening 30

Faerie Queen, The 54
Fairies 141
Fairies Banquet 28
Fairies dancing on the green by moonlight *110*, 111
Fairies flying over a cottage 39
Fairies in a bird's nest 127, *128*
Fairies in Tradition and Literature 66
Fairies, The 61
Fair Temple, The: or Oberon's Chapel 61-63
Fairy Banquet, The 127
Fairy Blackstick, The 68
Fairy Books 132
Fairy Connoisseurs, The 119
Fairy Family, The 132
Fairy Feller's Master Stroke, The 127
Fairy Garden, The 132
Fairy in an Autumn Glade 137
Fairy Legends and Traditions of the South of Ireland 117, 121
Fairy Library 117
Fairy Minuet, The *21*
Fairy Mythology, The 117, *118*
Fairy Queen, The 92, *92*
Fairy Raid, The *10*, 122
Fairy Ring, A *121*
Fairy Seated on a Mushroom *124*
Fairy Scene 59
Fairy's Rendezvous *18*
Fairy Stories (Andersen) 131, 139
Fairy Tales (Ritson) 67
Fairy Tales of the South of Ireland 67
Fantasia 140
Fantasy, A 119
Farfalla *109*
Faun and the Fairies, The *113*, 121
Feast, Michael 91, *91*
Ferdinand Lured by Ariel 130
Fians, Fairies and Picts 32
First of May, The: A Fairy Masque 132
Fitzgerald, John Anster 19, *28*, *46*, 127-128, *128*
Floral Fantasy in an Old English garden, A *12*, 132
Flora's Feast *20*, 132
Flora's Train 132
Flower Fairy in the Magic Garret, The *2*
Fokine, Michael 86, *86*, 106
Folk-Lore Society, The 32
Fonteyn, Margot *104*, 106, *106*
Ford, Henry Justice 132, *132*
Four Fairies Riding on Insects 65
Frauds on the Fairies 69
Friar Bacon and Friar Bungay 51
Fuseli, Henry 112, *112*
Fyleman, Rose 70

Gardner, E.L. 33, 37, 40
German Popular Stories 67, *114*, 117
Gervase of Tilbury 25
Gielgud, John 88, 91, *91*
Gilbert, John Selwyn 105
Gilbert, W.S., and Sullivan, A. 96, *98*
Giraldus Cambrensis 23-25
Goble, Warwick 140
Goblin Market 70, *130*, 131
Godwin, Fay *22*, *23*, *24*, *25*
Goodall, Frederick 59
Goring, Marius 88, *88*
Gower, John 49

Graham, Edith 14
Grahn, Lucile 103, 104
Granville-Barker, Harley 72, 80
Green Children 27
Greene, Robert 51
Griffiths, Frances 33, 34, 36
Grimm, the Brothers 67, 117
Grimshaw, John Atkinson 13
Griset, E. 120
Grisi, Carlotta 101
Guthrie, Tyrone 86

Hall, Peter 91, 91
Happy Prince, The 137
Hayman, Francis 111
Hay-Petrie, B. 86
Heatherley, Thomas 124, 125
Helpmann, Robert 87, 87, 92, 106, 106
Herrick, Robert 28, 60, 61
Hesperides 61
Hill, Octavius 125
Hobbit, The 71
Hobgoblin laughed till his sides ached,
    The 132
Hogarth, William 111
Hogg, James 26
Hop o' my Thumb 69
Horton, Priscilla 75, 75
Housman, Laurence 131
Howard, Alan 90
Hughes, Arthur 129, 130, 130
Huskisson, Robert 58, 122, 127
Huon of Bordeaux 50, 74

In Fairyland 70, 129, 134
Ingram, W.R. 71
Inman, Dorothy 37, 41
Iolanthe, or the Peer and Peri 96, 98
Iris 13
Irish Fairy and Folk Tales (Yeats) 41, 68
Irish Melodies 68, 121
Island of Jewels, The 101, 101
Itinerarium Cambriae 23
Ivanov, Lev 105

Jack and the Beanstalk 69
Jack Courting the Fairy 19
Jacob 140
Jacobs, Joseph 132
Jacobs, Sally 90
James I 72
James IV 51
James VI 57
Jeffries, Anne 28
Jones, Inigo 72, 73, 93, 111
Jonson, Ben 60, 72, 111
Joy, S.M. 103

Kean, Charles 77, 78
Keats, John 67
Keightley, Thomas 117, 118
Kestelman, Sara 90
Kilmeny 26
King, Jessie M. 2, 140
King of the Golden River, The 43, 53, 69,
    129
King Orfeo 31
Kipling, Rudyard 18, 19, 45, 70
Kirk, Robert 33, 111
Lamb, Charles and Mary 62
Lambert, Constant 92
Lamb's Tales from Shakespeare 138
Lang, Andrew 67, 71, 132, 132
Lees-Milne, James 41
Leigh, Vivien 87, 87
Leighton, Margaret 89
Lemon, Mark 119

Little Gentleman, The 120
Loeber, Vivien 107
Lord of the Rings, The 71
Luck of Edenhall, The 16, 16
Lyly, John 52, 56
Lynch, J.H. 102

Macdonald, George 69
Macdonald, Margaret and Frances 140
Mackintosh, Charles Rennie 140, 141
Maclaren, Archibald 132
Maclise, Daniel 112, 113, 116, 120
MacReady, William 74
MacRitchie, David 32
Maeterlinck, Maurice 138
Maids of Elfin Mere, The 70, 131
Makeig-Jones, Daisy 136, 137
Malory, Sir Thomas 50
Map, Walter 26
Marie de France 44
Marriot, William 38
Mary Rose 70
May Blossom, or the Princess and Her
    People, The 40
Maydes Metamorphosis, The 59-60
Meades, Emily 17
Meadows, Kenny 52, 54, 55
Memoirs of Bartholomew Fair 28
Mendelssohn, Felix 80, 85, 86, 95
Merlin 50, 112
Merry Wives of Windsor, The 56
Messel, Oliver 86, 88, 106
Metamorphoses 74
Middleton, Christopher 60
Midsummer Fairies 138
Midsummer Night's Dream, A 8, 13, 17,
    28, 33, 48, 51-54, 52, 54, 55, 59, 74-95, 76,
    77, 78, 79, 85, 86, 87, 90, 94, 116, 119, 121,
    123, 125, 139, 139
Midsummer Night's Fairies 127
Millais, John Everett 130
Millar, H.R. 18
Milton, John 64, 111
Minstrelsy of the Scottish Border 68
Moonlit Scene with Faeries 14
Moore, Thomas 68, 121
More Knaves Yet? The Knaves of Spades
    and Diamonds 60
Morgan le Fay 50
Morley, Henry 28, 77
Morris, William 69
Morte d'Arthur 50
Morton, Edward 103
Mother's Blessing, The 122
Music Masters, a love story, and two series
    of Day and Night Songs, The 70, 130,

Neilson, Julia 79, 80
Neues Deutsches Märchenbuch 56
Nimphidia, the Court of Fayrie 60
Nimuë 50, 112
Nutcracker, The 105
Nymph of Malham Cove, The,
    'Moonlight Idyll' 125

Oberon (Weiland) 96
Oberon: or the Elf-King's Oath 96, 97
Oberon's Diet 61
Oberon's Palace 61
Oberon, the Fairy Prince 60, 72, 73, 111
Oberon, Titania and Puck with Fairies
    Dancing 114, 115
Of Ghosts and Goblins 60
Olaus Magnus of Uppsala 111
Otia Imperiali 25
Outhwaite, Ida 140
Ovid 74

Pandemonium or the Devil's Cloister 111
Paracelsus 14, 57, 58
Paradise Lost 64
Pastime and Recreation of the Queen of the
    Fairies in Fairyland, the Centre of the
    Earth 64
Paton, Sir Joseph Noel 10, 15, 112, 116,
    120-122, 125, 129
Pears, Peter 93
Peele, George 51
Perrault, père et fils 67, 105
Perrot, Jules 103, 104
Peter Pan 42, 70, 107, 139, 140
Petipa, Marius 105, 106
Pink Fairy Book, The 132
Piper, John 93, 94
Planché, J.R. 96, 101
Poems and Fancies (Cavandish) 63
Pogány, Willy 42, 65, 140
Pope, Alexander 66, 116
Popular Nursery Tales including Tom
    Thumb 51
Principles and the Goblin, The 69
Proper New Ballad: The Fairies Farewell, A
    66
Psyche 17
Puck Fleeing before the Dawn 49, 111-112,
    139, 140
Puck of Pook's Hill 18, 19, 45, 70
Pursuit of Pleasure, The 15
Puss in Boots 67

Quarrel of Oberon and Titania, The 121
Queen Mab 66
Queen Summer or the Tournament of the
    Rose 132
Rackham, Arthur 45, 48, 137, 138, 139,
Ralph of Coggleshall 27
Rape of the Lock, The 66, 116
Raphael 17
Reconciliation of Oberon and Titania, The
    116, 121-122
Reynolds, Sir Joshua 111-112
Richardson, Ralph 87
Ritson, Joseph 64, 67
Robin Goodfellow, His Mad Pranks and
    Merry Jests 111
Robinson, Charles 137, 137, 140
Robinson, Frederick Cayley 138
Robinson, W. Heath 8, 137-140, 139
Romance of King Orfeo, The 44
Romeo and Juliet 52
Romney, George 116
Roscoe, William, M.P. 68
Rose and the Ring, The 68, 69
Rossetti, Christina 69-70, 129, 130, 130
Rossetti, Dante Gabriel 130, 131, 131
Rowlands, Samuel 60, 64
Ruskin, John 43, 53, 69, 129
Ryall, Henry Thomas 15

Sackville, Edward, 2nd Earl of Dorset 60
Sad Shepherd, The 60
Sainthill, Loudon 89
Schaufuss, Peter 107
Schiller, Friedrich von 66
Scott, David 31, 49
Scott, Reginald 54
Scott, Sir Walter 68
Secret Commonwealth of Elves, Fauns and
    Fairies, The 33
Selden, John 66
Shackleton, William 125
Sharp, Cecil 65
Shelley, Percy B. 66
Sibley, Antoinette 95

Simeon, Harry *18*
Simmons, John *53, 123*, 125
Sing Song, A Nursery Rhyme Book *129, 130, 130*
Sketches of Irish Characters 55
Sleeping Beauty, The 100, 105-106, *106*
Sleeping Beauty, The, and The Beast 99-101
Sleeping Princess, The 105, 106
Snow-Queen, The 132
Snow White 140
Songe de la Fantasie 126, 127
Spenser, Edmund 54
Sprites on a Cliff 127
Story Without an End, The 133
Stothard, Thomas 116
Strapola, Giovanni 67
Sylphide, La 102, 106
Sylphides, Les 106, 107

Table Talk 66
Taglioni, Marie 101-102, *102*
Tarrant, Margaret 19, 139, 140
Tchaikovsky, P.I. 105, 106
Tempest, The 56, 74-91, *75, 78, 88, 89, 91*

Terry, Ellen 77-78, *78*
Terry, Kate 79
Testimony of Tradition, The 32
Thackeray, William M. *68,* 69
There Sleeps Titania 58
Thomas the Rhymer 44
Titania *53*, 139, 140
Titania and Bottom 112, *112*
Titania, Puck and the Changeling 116
Titania's Awakening 112
Tolkien, J.R.R. 44, 71
Tom Pouce ou le Petit Garçon 50
Tom Thumbe, His Life and Death 58
Traditions of the Borders of the Tamar and the Tavey 67
Tree and Leaf 44
Tree, Herbert Beerbohm 79-80
Triumphal March of the Elf-King 134
Trumbully, William, the Elder 73

Udine 121
Utrecht Psalter, The 110

Valois, Ninette de 86
Vestris, Mme 76, *76*
Villanis *109*

Wallenstein 66
Water Babies, The 137
Watersprites in a Stream 65
Weber, Carl Maria von 96, *97*
Weiland 96
When the Spring Begins 133
Widow Whitgift and Her Sons, The 45
Wife of Bath's Tale, The 14, 31, 49
Wilcoxson, F.J. 27
Wild Edric 26
Wilde, Oscar 137
Wilhelm, Charles *100*
William of Newbridge 27
Wingrave, Marion *40*
Wood, J. Hickory 99
Wright, Elsie 33, *34, 35, 36, 37, 39,* 40
Wynkyn de Worde 50

Yeats, W.B. 41, 68, 70
Young, David 74

BIBLIOGRAPHY

Literature and Folklore
BRIGGS, K.M. *The Anatomy of Puck.* Routledge & Kegan Paul (1959).
BRIGGS, K.M. *The Fairies in Tradition and Literature.* Routledge & Kegan Paul (1967).
BRIGGS, K.M. *A Dictionary of Fairies.* Penguin Books (1976).
LATHAM, M.W. *Elizabethan Fairies.* (New York, 1930).
TOLKIEN, J.R.R. *Tree and Leaf.* George Allen & Unwin (1964).

Art
JOHNSON, D. *Fantastic Illustration and Design in Britain, 1850-1930.* Catalogue of an exhibition held at The Rhode Island School of Design (1979).
MAAS, J.S. *Victorian Painters.* Barrie & Rockliff (1969).
PHILLPOTTS, B. *Fairy Painting.* Ash & Grant (1978).

Theatre
BOOTH, M. (editor). *English Plays of the Nineteenth Century,* volume 5. Oxford University Press (1976).
GUEST, I. *The Romantic Ballet in England.* Phoenix House (1954).
MERCHANT, W.M. *Shakespeare and the Artist.* Oxford University Press (1959).
ODELL, G.C. *Shakespeare from Betterton to Irving.* Constable (1921).